The Greenleaf Guide to Old Testament History

by Robert G. Shearer
& Cynthia A. Shearer

Greenleaf Press
Lebanon, Tennessee

Internet: www.greenleafpress.com
3761 Highway 109N, Unit D
Lebanon, Tennessee 37087
615-449-1617

For orders only, call: 1-800-311-1508

History for the thoughtful child

Table of Contents

Lessons: Each lesson is intended to be read and discussed at one sitting. The questions are intended to be a guide for recall and discussion. They test comprehension and attempt to point out significant facts, events, people, and places.

    Deuteronomy, chapters 19-25 are more detailed laws given by Moses to govern Israel after settlement in the promised land. You may decide (especially with older children) that it is worthwhile to read through these. God's principles of justice are eternal and there is much for us to learn from these practical principles. Chapter 26 is a benediction on the law. Chapter 27-30 is a recitation of the blessings and curses which God sets before Israel in conjunction with keeping or disobeying the law. Again, you may choose to read these chapters in their entirety. We include a reading of chapters 29-30 as a lesson to summarize the blessings and curses associated with the law.

The last five chapters of the book of Judges tell the story of Micah, his household idols, and a live-in Levite priest; then the story of a Levite, his unfaithful concubine, the lawless men of Gibeah in Benjamin's land, and the resulting civil war among the 12 tribes. The stories and lessons are obscure and we have made the decision to omit them from this study. They do not seem to follow chronologically in the story of the Judges, but rather seem to be told to illustrate the principle "There was no king in Israel and each man did what was right in his own eyes. (17:6; 21:25). While all scripture is inspired and profitable, we think these sections are best left for another time, perhaps when your children are older and want to do a more detailed study of Israel's history between Egypt and King Saul - the period of the Judges.

Now we come to the books of 1 & 2 Samuel which tell the stories of the last two Judges, Eli & Samuel and the first two kings, Saul and David.

Kings and Chronicles tell overlapping stories in the Bible. 1 Chronicles begins with 10 chapters of genealogies going back to Abraham and then picks up with the death of Saul and the reign of David. 2 Chronicles recounts the reigns of Solomon and the succeeding Kings of Judah. The author of Chronicles does not deal with the Kings of Israel directly. Kings opens with the accession of Solomon (the stories of Samuel, Saul, and David are told in 1 & 2 Samuel) and then traces the stories of the Kings of Judah as well as the Kings of Israel. In selecting readings for this guide, I have relied primarily on Chronicles for stories about the kings of Judah and Kings for the kings of Israel. Almost all of the passages about the Kings of Judah in the books of 1 &2 Kings have parallels in Chronicles, but very little of what Kings has to say about the Kings of Israel is included. I have followed the sequence of kings as they are mentioned in the book of Kings.

For more information about:

        Alexander the Great
        Antiochus Epiphanes, and the Maccabees
        Herod the Great

I refer readers to ***Josephus, The Essential Writings***, by Paul L. Maier. Josephus is a fascinating writer and his work provides fascinating coverage of the history of Israel during the time between Old & New Testaments.

Introduction

This book was written to guide parents in introducing the history of Israel to their children. It is our conviction that children should be acquainted with the Bible as early as is practical. We are convinced that the stories from the Old Testament are given to us to teach us and our children important lessons about godliness and wisdom.

Whenever we have talked about teaching history to children, we have encouraged families to make the history of Israel, the Old Testament, their children's first history. It has not mattered where we are — we can always count on seeing one of three reactions from our listeners. Some look at us as if we are crazy: "What else **would** you start with, we've been doing that all along." Some look at us as if we are crazy: "Sure, we'd like to teach the Bible to our children, but surely you don't mean **young** children. It's too hard!" And the rest look at us as if we are crazy. In fact, this group often tells us we are crazy. They say "You don't expect me to teach the Old Testament to **children** — **I** can't even understand the Old Testament."

As a people, we do not really know the Scriptures very well. And we have forgotten that God has commanded, not merely suggested, that we pass on these things (these Old Testament stories) to our children. Sometimes we are overwhelmed, paralyzed by a realization of our own shortcomings. So very often, we honestly do not know where to start. And sadly, with few exceptions, our churches are not helping us very much.

As we have read through the story of Israel again this time, we have been most struck by something we already knew — but have seen again. We have been painfully reminded of the fact that we truly are always only one generation away from a return to paganism. This is true and demonstrated all the way through the history of Israel, the history of the Church, and is in evidence in our own churches (and I mean the good, solid, doctrinally-correct churches that most of us seek out). We are not immune.

The pattern runs something like this: Parents are blessed by God and set about to enjoy the blessings. Children remember that their parents were blessed by God and continue to enjoy the blessings. Grandchildren enjoy the blessings and forget their source. And all of a sudden we have a generation who know neither Joseph or his God. God becomes for them some small part of their cultural identity — something like the state bird or flower. They know there is one, but its existence really doesn't trouble them very much.

This pattern is played out over and over again throughout the history of Israel. A history of a people who, for the most part, keep forgetting who their God is and what He has done for them. Our deepest fear and sadness is that the same pattern is being played out again within the believing Church today. If we do not pass on to our children our own love for and delight in the Word of God; if we allow the Sunday School or youth group to become the primary source of Biblical instruction; if in our home instruction, we make the Word of God a slave to workbook pages and fill in the blank lessons, we will lose our children. Our believing churches (for all their doctrinal soundness) are producing a generation of children who, for all their head knowledge, have no heart for God.

However, we do not believe that such an outcome is inevitable. The good news is that we can as adults, fall in love with the Word of God. We can infect our children with a love for the Word if we will just let the Bible speak for itself. Tell its stories as if they are real, living stories. Read them with the same loving expression that we use when we read our favorite family read-alouds. We should be able to laugh just a little as the angel announces to a cowering Gideon, "Hail, mighty man of valor!" We should cheer David on as he confronts Goliath in the name of the Living God. We should feel the sadness that David feels as he realizes that his best friend, Jonathan, is dead. And we should rejoice with God's people in Susa as God delivers them from the hand of wicked Haman.

If we find delight in the Word, for the most part, our children will follow. If we approach it with fear and uncertainty, we can be sure our children will follow our lead here, too. With the psalmist we need to call our children to join us, to "Taste and see that the Lord is Good!"

And that's the basic purpose behind this book. It is intended to be a guide to help you, as parents, to organize your study of the Old Testament with your children.

This book is not a commentary. It will not answer all your questions about the Old Testament. We have concentrated on the historical narratives, telling where the laws and the prophets fit into the history, but we concentrate on the historical books themselves. This is a source book for a basic historical overview. Once you have given your children the big picture, you will want to continue through the Gospels and Acts. And then, once they grasp the stories and the major themes, you will want to show them how to camp out in the Scriptures — learn how to inductively study the Word for themselves. We strongly recommend that your Bible instruction go far beyond the scope of this guide. We hope that the study you begin with your children here will only be the beginning of a lifelong passion for the Word of God that will produce a generation of believers like those described by Daniel 11.32 — a people who know their God, are strong and do great things.

How to Use this Book

The readings from the Bible outlined here are selected for the purpose of studying the history of Israel. The focus is on history — not theology. The audience intended are children — not adults. The focus is always on one or two central characters, Repeatedly, we will ask, "What actions are worthy of imitation?" "What actions should we avoid?" "What is God's judgment on this life?"

The focus is on understanding God's providential action and intervention through history, guiding the destiny of the children of Israel. Like the Famous Men series (with titles on Egypt, Greece, Rome, Middle Ages, Renaissance & Reformation) which follows it, this history unit is built around a series of biographies. We have not attempted to write a Famous Men of the Old Testament book, since one already exists, and we don't presume to suppose that we could improve upon it (the Bible!).

The 196 readings are intended to be used, one each day throughout the school year. Yes, we know that's a few more readings than most people have school days. Be creative. You could do more than one reading on some days, or you could continue the study into the summer or the next school year. We really tried to fit Old Testament History into 180 readings, but we just couldn't do it and we couldn't bear to leave anything out.

The readings are designed to give the student (and parent/teacher) an overview of the history of Israel and an introduction to the key figures whose lives God uses to teach us about Himself and His character. These stories are intended for children in the elementary grades, and should be accessible, even to children in kindergarten or first grade. (Actually, anyone of any age wanting to get an overview of Old Testament history might find this book to be helpful.) If this seems surprising, the reader is reminded that God's plan for families is for fathers to teach these stories to their children. When God decrees in Deuteronomy 6:6-7 that "you shall teach them diligently to your sons and shall talk of them when you sit in your house and when you walk by the way and when you lie down and when you rise up," he is not referring to math facts and grammar rules. God's textbook for children are the stories from the Old Testament. He is specifically referring here to the story of the Exodus from Egypt, but by implication he means the entire Old Testament. The Old Testament is God's textbook for children. It is the only textbook, quite probably, which Jesus used during his education in the house of his parents (and perhaps with a rabbi in Nazareth).

For each reading, we recommend the following outline:

Pray

Review

Read-aloud

Narrate

Discuss

Pray

As a teaching technique, we heartily commend to you a practice described as narration by Charlotte Mason (for more about her educational philosophies, see **For the Children's Sake** by Susan Schaeffer Macaulay and **The Original Home Education Series** by Charlotte Mason). Narration is a simple technique in which the child reads or listens to a story and then is asked to tell the story back in his own words. This exercise is difficult at first, but over time (actually a short time) the child will learn to focus his attention and remember significant details so that he can retell what he has learned. It is important not to do too much prompting or correcting and not to offer the child a second reading too readily. Begin with short passages (a paragraph or two) and before long, your child will be able to recount passages of 3-4 pages (about 5-10 minutes worth of out-loud reading).

After giving his own narration back to you (this is your check to make sure he has comprehended the passage), use the discussion questions as a guide to help focus on significant events, ideas, and lessons in each passage.

After you have read the passage out loud, have your students tell the story back to you. If you have more than one student, then have them alternate telling the story as you call on them. This will keep the attention of those who are NOT at the moment narrating from wandering.

From the start, train your students to listen for answers to the basic questions that begin with the words who, what, when, where, why, and how. This simple habit is a foundational study skill (for any study) and is especially important for inductive Bible study.

Teaching Aids

Maps, coloring books, flannel graphs, puzzles, story tapes, animated video versions all have their place (though with regard to audios and videos - be scrupulously fanatical about accuracy). Any or all of these may prove helpful with your child. None of these will catch their interest and work ALL of the time. If you notice their eyes glazing over, stop. Don't push them too hard. This is supposed to be fun.

Dates

The dates we have used are those generally agreed upon by conservative scholars. If you have a King James Bible with Bishop Ussher's dates (an Irish Bishop who worked out a system of dates for the Old Testament in the 19th century), then you will find substantial agreement. Other conservative scholars may vary somewhat. For the later time periods of the Old Testament, there is little controversy. The regnal dates of Saul, David, and Solomon are confirmed by records from other contemporary cultures that mention them. The further back in time you go from Saul however, the greater the divergence of opinion. The largest area of controversy concerns the dating of the Exodus.

In the 19th century, critical (read that skeptical and quite often heretical) scholars began to express doubts about the traditional dating of the Exodus. They argued, for example, that Moses could not have developed the law and his monotheistic emphasis as early as had been supposed. He must, they argued, have picked these ideas up from later developments in Egyptian history. In particular, the critics argued that Moses drew heavily on Ahknaton, the monotheistic pharaoh whose reign was from 1361 B.C. to 1344 B.C.

But the skeptics' arguments beg the question. They assume Moses' ideas were derived from Egyptian culture, therefore they move his dates to a much later period, then they point to the earlier Egyptian ideas as their "proof" that Moses "borrowed" his best ideas. It is all a fairly transparent and calculated attempt to cast doubt on the authority of the Bible.

But if God is who He claims He is, does it not make sense that His giving of the law would be a unique event, without immediate antecedents? And if Egypt was rocked by plagues and a military disaster during the Exodus, would it be unusual if that brought about a turning away from the traditional Egyptian gods and the rise of a group seeking the truth about one true God. Seen in this light, the reforms of Pharaoh Ahknaton are a sign that the Exodus had a spiritual impact on Egypt.

Graphical Timeline of Ancient History

by Robert G. Shearer
© 1996 Greenleaf Press

Key Dates

Israel
c.1900 B.C. –	Joseph sold into slavery
c.1445 B.C. –	The Exodus
c.1000 B.C. –	Death of Saul, David becomes King
605-1344 B.C. –	The Exile

Egypt
2500 B.C. –	Khufu (Cheops) The Great Pyramid
1505-1484 B.C. –	Queen Hatshepsut
1361-1344 B.C. –	Amenhotep IV also known as Akhenaton
51-31 B.C. –	Cleopatra

Greece
c.1200 B.C. –	Siege of Troy
478-404 B.C. –	Civil War between Athens & Sparta
356-323 B.C. –	Alexander

Rome
753 B.C. –	Founding of Rome
509 B.C. –	Founding of the Roman Republic
100-44 B.C. –	Julius Caesar
312-327 A.D. –	Constantine
410 A.D. –	Sack of Rome by the Visigoths
476 A.D. –	Death of the last Roman Emperor

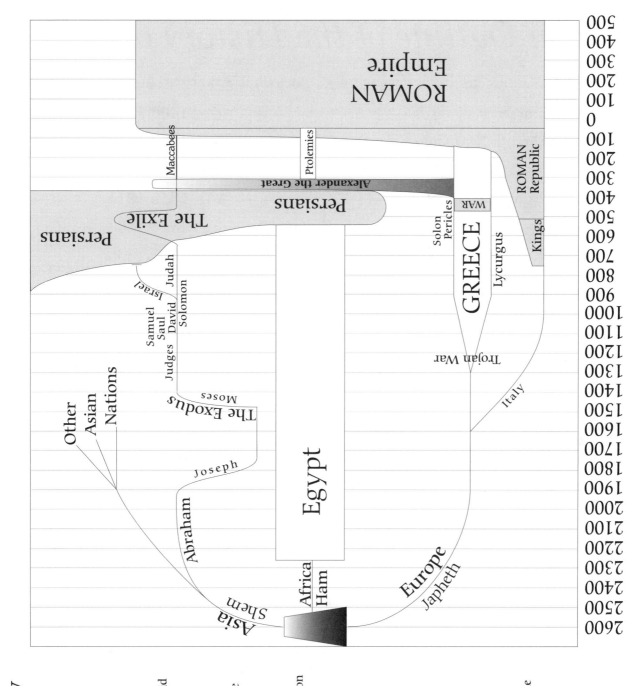

An Outline of the History of Israel

Most of us know instinctively the major periods of American history:

Explorers	1400-1600
Pilgrims and Colonists	1604-1750
The American Revolution	1750-1787
The War of 1812	1812-1815
Sectionalism and Westward Expansion	1815-1860
The War Between the States	1861-1865
Reconstruction	1865-1900
World War 1	1914-1921
The Great Depression	1929-1940
World War 2	1941-1945
The 50's, the 60's, etc.	1950-1990...

We should spend some time getting a firm outline of Israel's history.

The Patriarchs	2200-1700 B.C.
Slavery in Egypt	1700-1450 B.C.
The Exodus	1453 B.C.
Judges	1413-1020 B.C.
The United Kingdom	1051-931 B.C.
The Divided Kingdom (Israel & Judah)	931-586 B.C.
The Babylonian Exile	605-535 B.C.
The Return & Rebuilding	536-415 B.C.

On the preceding page is an overview of the history of Israel from the tower of Babel through the exile and return. The history of Israel is shown along the top line (the descendants of Shem). The development of other, neighboring civilizations are shown in the lines of Ham, and Japheth

---

Lesson 1
God Creates
Genesis 1:1-2:3

Background: *The first three chapters of scripture contain rich lessons for all of us. For children, it is important to establish for them that God is the creator of the entire universe, and of everything, and everyone in it.*

1.   When do the events of the passage happen?

2.   Who acts in the passage? Note any pronouns. Are they singular or plural? What significance might this have?

3.   You might want to make a chart with the words "Light, waters, earth, and dry land" and note what you learn about each.

     Notice how the 6 days divides into two groups of threes. In the first 3 days, God creates three realms, the heavens, the expanse between the waters, and the dry land. In the second 3 days God populates each of the realms: stars in the heavens, fish and birds in the skies and the waters, and finally animals and man on the dry land.

     Day 1: light and darkness
     Day 2: divison of the waters
     Day 3: dry land, seas, vegetation
     Day 4: stars, sun, & moon   (for the heavens)
     Day 5: fish and birds   (for the seas and the skies)
     Day 6: land animals, man   (for the dry land)

4.   What is God's opinion of His creation? How often is this judgement repeated?

5.   What is different about the creation of man from the creation of the animals?

     *Some families have found it profitable to organize the study of science around the days of creation. One resource for this is the book, **Science in the Creation Week** by Unfred.*

Lesson 2.
Adam and Eve
Genesis 2:4-3:24

Remember the outline: Pray, Review, Read, Narrate, Discuss, and Pray again.

1. Name those who are involved in the story told in 2:4-3:24

2. What do you learn about each one?

3. Where does this story take place?

4. What responsibility does God give to man? (2:15)

5. Who named the animals? (2:19)

6. Why was Eve created? How does her creation differ from the animals?

7. Look in more detail at the conversations between God and Adam in 2:15-17. Compare this with Satan's report in 3:1-6.

8. Where was Eve when God said these things? How would she have found out what God has said? Does she know what God said accurately?

9. Does the serpent repeat what God said accurately? (Try reading the two passages one after the other to your younger children and have them listen for the differences.)

10. What happened because Adam and Eve disobeyed?

11. Why is it silly to hide from God? Why is it "natural?"

12. Whom does God curse because of Adam and Eve's disobedience? How is the curse different for each of them?

    Don't overlook Genesis 3:15, generally understood to be the first prophecy of the messiah.

13. Why do you think Adam calls Eve the "mother of all the living?" Why wouldn't he name her "cursed woman God saddled me with?"

14. What does God do for Adam and Eve AFTER the fall? How are the clothes God makes for Adam and Eve different from the clothes they made for themselves? How is this a picture of our own redemption?

Lesson 3.
Cain and Abel
Genesis 4

1. Who was the older of the two brothers?

2. **Something to think about:** Is it possible that Eve thought Cain was the Messiah who would bruise the serpent's heel?

3. What was Cain's occupation?

4. What was Abel's occupation?

5. How would you describe Cain's relationship with Abel?

6. Is Cain able to hide his sin? What implications does this have for us?
   "The voice of your brother's blood is crying to Me from the ground..."

7. What happens to Cain because of Abel's murder? Why does God place a special mark on Cain?

   The rest of this chapter provides us with a history of Cain and his offspring. Our middle elementary children on up enjoyed making a genealogical chart of the people listed here. In addition to recording the names of the individuals, we also made note of any special accomplishments attributed to an individual. Our younger children (Kindergarten and first grade) bailed out before we got very deeply into this — so watch closely for the signals that say, "You may be enjoying this, but we're sure not!" In such cases it would probably be better for you to make the chart and share highlights with the kids briefly. Suggested highlights follow.

8. Notice when the men described in Genesis 4 do things like build cities, work with metals, play instruments, live in tents and raise cattle. Compare the sequence described in Genesis with the typical evolutionary scenario: "primitive man moves from caves to tents and follows animals to seasonal pastures for years and years and years, until he figures out how to build fences and houses and EUREKA! — cities!"

9. Be sure and ask your students to identify the specific offspring and the occupations they are noted for.

10. What is the name of Adam and Eve's third son?

Lesson 4.
Enoch and Methuselah
Genesis 5

Though at first, this chapter may appear to be one of those insufferable lists of who begat whom, don't be quick to skip it. Although your younger children may not be quite ready to walk through it in much detail, we would recommend that the parent or teacher at least do it themselves.

With our older children (3rd grade and up) we made a chart of Seth's descendants, noting names, ages of each father when his son was born, age of each man at his death. Out to the side of the chart, I kept a running tally of Adam's age — which will also give you, obviously, the amount of time MAN has been around.

*As I record Adam's age beside each name in the genealogy, I ask "Is Adam still alive?" And then I point out that Adam was indeed able to pass on a first hand account of life before and after The Fall to a long line of people. This activity seemed to help all of us see the early history of man in a new, very real light. It is possible to get the same information from the charts in **The International Inductive Study Bible** or **The Wallchart of World History**. However, there is something about doing the numbers yourself that will really make the information "yours". Thus, we recommend it, at least to you, if not to your children.*

For Discussion:

1. The phrase "These are the generations of..." is repeated throughout Genesis. Watch for it. (This is, in fact, its second appearance).

2. How many sons and daughters did Adam and Eve have? Which ones are specifically named? (see v. 4: "He had other sons and daughters ..." This is the answer to the proverbial question of skeptics, "where did Cain's wife come from?")

3. How is Enoch different from the other descendants of Adam? When does the text say Enoch died? (WARNING! WARNING! TRICK QUESTION!) What does it say about how Enoch ended his time among men? What does Enoch name his son?

Background: *Enoch was apparently one of the first prophets/preachers in the Word. A look at Jude, verses 14 & 15 will give you a description of what he preached. Read this to your children. Enoch not only preached against the wickedness of the world, but provided a prophetic word about coming judgement through the name of his son, Methuselah. Methuselah's name means, "after me, it comes." God confirms this prophetic word by withholding judgement until after Methuselah's death.*

It is possible to calculate the flood year as you keep a tally of the years which have passed since Adam's creation. When you run the numbers, you find that Methuselah died the year the flood began. Our kids were greatly impressed by this.

4. What did Enoch preach?

5. When does Adam die? How long after his death was Noah born? How could Noah's father have found out the details of life before and after The Fall?

6. What does Lamech prophesy about Noah? (verse 29)

Lesson 5.
The Earth had become Wicked
Genesis 6-7:5

Background: *The idea of angels (the sons of God) taking wives for themselves from among the daughters of men may not seem wicked to us at first, but it displeased God greatly. It appears to have violated his intentions for both angels and women. By the time described in verse five, man is thoroughly corrupt. It is hard to imagine a description of evil more depraved or complete.*

Verse 4 has been cited by many commentators as the historical background behind many of the myths told in other cultures about figures who were half-man, half-god.

1. What is man's condition and character?

   Try focusing on each aspect of God's pronouncement to emphasize its completeness.

   > *SOME of the intents of his heart?...........................no, EVERY intent*
   > *are a LITTLE bit bad? ....no, ONLY evil*
   > *SOME of the time?...no, CONTINUALLY*

2. God repeats his judgement on the earth as corrupt in v. 11, 12, and 13... What is the only specific charge made?

3. How does God respond to man's condition? What does this tell us about his character?

Application: *Remind your children that violence begins with and includes hitting and hurting each other intentionally no matter how old they are. Violence may increase in degree as we mature, but not in kind. Emphasize to your children how much God hates violence and cruelty — at any age.*

3. Verse 8 begins with "But Noah... " signaling a contrast. What is the contrast?

4. How does God describe Noah? How does this compare with how God described the world?
   Four things are recorded about Noah: he found favor in the eyes of the LORD; he was a righteous man; he was blameless in his time; he walked with God.

5. What does God tell Noah to do? What is Noah's response?

7. Was this just a local flood?
   "everything that is on the earth shall perish." verse 17

"Thus Noah did; according to all that God had commanded him, so he did."
Genesis 6:22

Lesson 6.
The Flood
Genesis 7 & 8

1. Did Noah wait until it started raining to enter the ark?

2. How many people were on the ark?

3. Who gathered the animals and who shut the door to the ark? (Check your picture books for accuracy!)

4. What would you say to someone who said, "This was only a local flood?"

5. How long did it rain?

6. Where else did water come from?

7. What two birds did Noah send out to find land?

8. What was the first thing Noah did after leaving the ark?

9. What promise did God make to Noah?

10. Every civilization has a flood myth. Why do you suppose this might be true?

Lesson 7.
The Rainbow and God's Covenant
Genesis 9

Reminder: *Pray, Review, Read aloud, Narrate, Discuss, Pray!*

1. After Noah leaves the ark, what does God command him to do first?

2. What new instructions concerning the animals does God give to Noah?

3. What is the relationship between man and the animals?

4. What punishment does God prescribe for murder?

5. This is the first mention of the word "covenant" in the Bible. What is a covenant? What are the terms of God's covenant with Noah?

6. What is the significance of the rainbow?

7. What foolish thing did Noah do?

8. How do the reactions of his sons differ?

9. What is the consequence of Ham's disrespect for his father?

Background: *Noah curses his son Ham and in his curse prophesies that Ham's descendants will serve the descendants of the other two. This prophecy was historically fulfilled in the conquest of Canaan (inhabited by Ham's descendants) by Shem's descendants, the Hebrews.*

Lesson 8.
The Tower of Babel
Genesis 11

1. What language did the descendants of Noah speak?

2. Why did men want to build the tower?

3. How does God react to the ambitions of men?

4. What happened? What two changes did God make among men?

5. Where did men go?

   The rest of chapter 11 traces the descendants of Shem down to Abram. Again, it is interesting to note who is a contemporary of whom. To keep the list of names and numbers from becoming a jumble, try charting each (go slowly, verse by verse). This is definitely an optional activity - it won't appeal to all children or families.

6. What do we learn about Abram's family in 11:26-32?

   Remember this section serves as background and overview for the story of Abram. The next fourteen chapters will fill in the details.

7. What do we learn about Abram? What kind of man is he? What sort of relationship does he have with his father? What do we know about his brother? his nephew? His wife?

8. Where does Abram travel? Plot his course on a map.

Maps: *The map #3 **The Student Bible Atlas** shows the course of Abram's journeys. Major cities mentioned in Genesis are also indicated. You will want to refer to this map several times during the next 5-10 lessons.*

*There is also a map on page 13 of **The Cultural Atlas of the Bible** which shows in more detail the routes of the patriarchs, Abraham, Isaac, and Jacob.*

Genesis 12-25

Fourteen chapters of the book of Genesis are concerned with Abraham. This represents almost a third of the entire book of Genesis.

Chapter 12 Abram called to leave his home, winds up in Egypt

Chapter 13 Lot & Abram divide the Negev

Chapter 14 Abram rescues Lot after he is taken prisoner

Chapter 15 God renews his promise to Abram

Chapter 16 Sarai gives Hagar to Abram producing Ishmael

Chapter 17 God renews his promise to Abram

Chapter 18 God visits Abraham on his way to destroy Sodom

Chapter 19 Lot saved from the destruction of Sodom

Chapter 20 Abraham, Sarah, and Abimelech (the Philistine king!)

Chapter 21 Sarah conceives and bears Isaac

Chapter 22 The sacrifice of Isaac

Chapter 23 The tomb of the patriarchs in Hebron

Chapter 24 Abraham sends his servant back to find a wife for Isaac

Chapter 25 The death of Abraham, the birth of Esau & Jacob

As you read, follow the action on a map whenever possible. ***The Student Bible Atlas, The Cultural Atlas of the Bible,*** or any good map of Bible times will do. It will help make it real for your children to see that the story is anchored in real geography.

As in all scripture, remember, opportunities to apply the truths in our own lives (whether we are 4, 14, or 40+) are endless. Ask the Holy Spirit to use the Word in your own life and the lives of your family members.

Lesson 9.

Abram called to leave his home, winds up in Egypt
Lot & Abram divide the Negev
Genesis 12 & 13

Follow the travels in this chapter on a map as you read aloud.

1. What does God command Abram to do? What does God promise Abram? What is Abram's response? How old was Abram?

2. What is Abram afraid will happen to him in Egypt? Why did he go to Egypt in the first place?

3. Did the Egyptians notice that Sarai was beautiful? What did they do?

4. Did Abram's scheme protect him from being killed? Did it protect Sarai?

5. What happened to Pharaoh's house because he had "married" Sarai?

6. What does Pharaoh do when he finds out that Abram had deceived him?

7. Abram ends up in the Negev after all. Question to ponder: Is there still a famine, or has he managed to avoid it?

8. Who is Lot? Were Abram and Lot rich? How rich? What problem did this cause?

9. What solution did Abram propose to Lot?

10. Why didn't Abram choose the best for himself and assign Lot to some portion?

11. Why does Lot choose the valley of the Jordan? What problems await Lot in the cities of the valley of the Jordan?

12. How bad were the men of Sodom?

Civil War in the Jordan Valley, Lot taken Prisoner

God renews his promise to Abram
Genesis 14 & 15

Background: *Verses 1-7 set the stage, giving the names of the kings and nations which ruled over the cities of the Jordan valley. Verses 8 & 9 describes the rebellion by 5 kings of the Jordan valley against 4 kings of the surrounding nations. Scholars are still unable to identify all of the kings and nations named here, though that is no reason for us to doubt that the events occurred as described. You could summarize the first 10 verses of the chapter with:*

"There was a civil war between the kings of Sodom and Gomorrah and the kings of the surrounding lands. The kings of the surrounding lands won a battle and captured Sodom and Gomorrah and took plunder and prisoners."

In these two chapters look especially at forms of the word, "possess." Who possesses and who gives?

1. When Abram hears that Lot has been taken prisoner, what does he do?

2. How far does he pursue Lot's captors in order to free him? Find Sodom and Gomorrah on a map and review the distance to Damascus. How long would it take on foot to travel?

3. Who is Melchizedek? What do you learn about him? What are Melchizedek's two titles?

4. What does Melchizedek do when he meets Abram?

5. What reward does the king of Sodom offer Abram?

6. Why does Abram refuse to take money?

   What application can be made to our own lives here? Contrast the rewards offered by the King of Sodom in 14:21 and by God in 15:1. Which rewards are you seeking? Who are you seeking a reward from?

Lesson 10.
Civil War in the Jordan Valley,
Lot taken Prisoner
God renews his promise to Abram
Genesis 14 & 15
(continued)

7. What does God promise Abram in chapter 15?

Background: *Verse 6 is one of the most frequently cited verses in the Bible.*

"Then he believed in the LORD; and He reckoned it to him as righteousness"

Verse 6 is central for the writer of Hebrews, for Paul in the book of Romans, and for Augustine and Luther as they sought to understand how God saves. Your older students might want to take some time out at this point to look at Romans 4, Hebrews 11, and/or Galatians 3.

8. Was Abram counted righteous because of what he had done?

Background: *The covenant or solemn promise from God to Abram is accompanied by what seems to us to be strange symbolism. It was the custom of the times, when two parties made a covenant or solemn promise, to sacrifice animals and divide them and then proclaim "so may it be done to him who breaks this covenant." Abram has nothing to offer to God except his own trust and belief (v.6). God commits to make Abram a great nation and to give him the land of Canaan.*

Prophecy: *God foretells that Abram's descendants will be strangers in a land that is not theirs and will be enslaved and oppressed for 400 years. This prophecy has its fulfillment when Joseph and then his brothers move to Egypt and eventually become slaves.*

Maps: *Find the river of Egypt (the Nile) and the Euphrates river on a map. God sets these two rivers as the boundaries of the land he is giving to Abram and his descendants. On a modern map of the Near East, mark these boundaries. What modern countries fall within these borders?*

Lesson 11.
Sarai gives Hagar to Abram
God renews his promise to Abram
Genesis 16 & 17

Background: *Neither Sarai nor Abram seem to have fully understood what God had promised to do. It has been 10 years since Abram first heard and obeyed God's call to leave Haran and move to Canaan. He has been promised an heir, but Sarai is still barren.*

Chapter 16

1. How much time has passed since God established a covenant with Abram?

2. What is Hagar's reaction to her new status (she has gone from being Sarai's maid to being Abram's wife) and the fact that she is now carrying Abram's child?

3. Why does Sarai treat Hagar harshly?

4. What does God promise to Ishmael? What kind of person does God say Ishmael will be? What sort of nation will Ishmael give rise to?

Chapter 17

5. How much time has passed since the last chapter?

6. Why does God change Abram's name? What does his new name mean?

7. What is the significance of circumcision? Does circumcision change a child's status with God?

Note: *Please explain circumcision to your children. When we were in college, each year without fail, there was always some innocent freshman girl in each small group Bible study who stopped everyone dead in their tracks with the dreaded question, "What is circumcision?"*

8. How did Abraham react to the news that Sarah would have a child?

9. How long after God's command did Abraham wait to institute circumcision as the sign of the covenant? Who did Abraham direct should be circumcised?

Lesson 12.
God visits Abraham
on his way to destroy Sodom
Genesis 18

1. Abraham knows that his visitors are from God. How does he treat them?

2. What message do the visitors' bring to him?

3. What does Sarah do when she hears the news?
   see Hebrews 11:11 to clear up the matter of Sarah's faith.

4. Why does God say that he has chosen Abraham? (verse 19)

5. What does God say about Sodom and Gomorrah? How will he respond? Why is he telling Abraham what he is about to do?

6. How does God respond to Abraham's questions? What do we learn about the character of God in this chapter?

   If there are 50 righteous will you spare the city?
   If there are 45?
   If there are 40?
   If there are 30?
   If there are 20?
   If there are 10?
   Now for the question: Will God find 10 righteous men in Sodom?
   (Remember: Sodom is where Lot and his family live...)

Lesson 13.
Lot in Sodom
Genesis 19

1. Where do the angels find Lot? What does this detail reveal about him?

Background: *"Sitting in the gate" means he was one of the influential leaders of the city. Those who "sat in the gate" were informal judges to whom one could bring civil cases and legal disputes for resolution.*

2. How does Lot treat the two angels? Did he recognize that they were angels?

Background: *To understand a bit more about Lot and his behavior in Sodom, we need to turn to a passage in the New Testament, 2 Peter 2:7-8 ("Lot, oppressed by the sensual conduct of unprincipled men... ")*

3. How did Lot feel about the wickedness of Sodom?

4. How did the men of Sodom demonstrate their wickedness?

Note: *It is not necessary to go into detail about what the men of Sodom wanted to do to the angels and Lot's daughters. The evil, sinister nature of the men comes through a plain reading of the text clearly. Children tend to shrink from the characters, horrified that they want to hurt (and hurt is what is primarily communicated) God's angels and Lot's daughters.*

5. Why did Lot's sons-in-law not come with him? What does this reveal about Lot?

6. What did God do to the cities of Sodom and Gomorrah?

7. What happened to Lot's wife?

8. Why was Lot saved? (verse 29)

Note: *verses 30-38 tell the story of Lot's relations with his daughters and the origins of the Moabites and the Ammonites. You might decide to skip over this section, or summarize it briefly.*

Lesson 14.
Abraham, Sarah, and Abimelech
Sarah conceives and bears Isaac
Genesis 20-21

Chapter 20

1. How old is Sarah? What does Abraham say about her to Abimelech? Why would Abimelech want to marry her?

2. How did Abimelech discover that Sarah was not Abraham's sister?

3. What does Abimelech's conversation reveal about his relationship with God?

4. How does God describe Abraham in his conversation with Abimelech?

5. What explanation does Abraham give Abimelech for his actions?

6. What had God done to the household of Abimelech as long as Sarah was there?

Chapter 21

Background: *Abraham laughed, Sarah laughed, so they named their son, "Laughter." (that is literally what Isaac means!)*

7. What does Sarah's choice of a name tell us about her?

8. What was Ishmael's attitude toward his half-brother, Isaac?

9. What does Sarah ask Abraham to do?

10. What does God advise Abraham to do?

11. How does God deal with Hagar and Ishmael?

12. Why does Abimelech approach Abraham? Who is more powerful politically and militarily? What does Abimelech's request reveal about his relationship with God?

13. How does Abimelech deal with Abraham's complaint?

The Sacrifice of Isaac

The death and burial of Sarah in the tomb of the patriarchs in Hebron
Genesis 22 & 23

Chapter 22

1. What does God do to test Abraham? How is God's call to Abraham different on this occasion?

2. How could Abraham obey God, sacrifice Isaac, and still believe that God would fulfill his promise?

Background: *For more insight on Abraham's actions, read Hebrews 11:17-19. According to Hebrews, Abraham believed that God would raise Isaac from the dead. Are there clues in the Genesis account which hint at what Abraham believed?*

3. Does Abraham pass the test?

Background: *It is interesting to note the repetition of the phrase, "your son, your only son." What God asks of Abraham is what he himself will offer in the sacrifice of the messiah.*

Another interesting repetition is Abraham's answer "Here I am" to God, Isaac, and the angel of the LORD. It is both an anticipation of the response of later prophets (from Moses to Isaiah) and an echo of God's own name ("I AM").

Chapter 23

4. How old was Sarah when she died?

5. Where did Abraham bury her?

Background: *The death of Sarah is the occasion for Abraham to acquire ownership for the first time of land in Canaan. The cave near Mamre is still a revered site for Jews, known as the tomb of the Patriarchs in the city of Hebron.*

Lesson 16.
Abraham sends for a wife for Isaac
Genesis 24

Background: *This is a long chapter, the longest in the book of Genesis! Part of the reason for the length is that the meeting between Rachel and Abraham's servant at the well is described three times: once prophetically; once as it happens; and once as it is retold by the servant to Rebekah's brother, Laban.*

1. Why does Abraham send his servant back to Mesopotamia to find a wife for Isaac from among his own people?

2. What does Abraham tell his servant to do and not to do? Why does he forbid him to take Isaac back?

3. Rebekah agrees to give Abraham's servant a drink of water. What else does she offer to do? Do you think this would normally be woman's work? (another question: What kind of a gentleman would let her do this?)

4. After Laban is told of the meeting and Abraham's servant indicates the miraculous circumstances, he immediately agrees to allow Rebekah to return to Canaan to marry Isaac. Why does he agree so easily? Do you think he is impressed with Abraham's wealth? With the prophetic circumstances of Rebekah's meeting?

5. Were you surprised when Rebekah says immediately, "I will go." Why is her answer unexpected?

6. Isaac and Rebekah seem to experience "love at first sight." Do you think it was coincidence that Isaac was out in the field meditating when Rebekah came into sight on her camel?

Lesson 17.

The death of Abraham
The birth of Esau and Jacob
The transfer of the birthright
Genesis 25

"Abraham died in a ripe old age, an old man and satisfied with life..." **Genesis 25:8**

1. Who buried Abraham? Where? Who else had been buried there?

2. Where did Ishmael's descendants settle? What was the attitude of his relatives?

3. Rebekah at first was barren... In what way was she able to conceive?

4. How are Jacob and Esau described before their birth? Compare their behavior before their births with behavior afterwards. *For more Biblical commentary on the character of the unborn, see also Psalm 139.*

"And the older shall serve the younger..." **Genesis 25:23**

5. How do Jacob and Esau differ as they grow up?

6. How did their parents differ in the way they treated them?

7. How does Esau describe his condition to Jacob when he comes in from the field? Do you think it's accurate or exaggerated? Why?

8. How does Jacob take advantage of the situation? Would you say he really "tricks" Esau into selling his birthright?

9. What does Esau's willingness to sell his birthright tell you about him?

"Thus Esau despised his birthright." **Genesis 25:34**

Lesson 18.
Like father, like son
Genesis 26

1. What does God tell Isaac NOT to do in avoiding the famine? What promise does God make to Isaac?

Background: *This Abimelech is not necessarily the same one who mistakenly took Sarah into his harem. The name may be a dynastic family who ruled the Philistines for several generations.*

2. Why does Isaac lie about Rebekah? Should he have known better?

3. How was Isaac's lie discovered?

Background: *in verse 8, the word translated "caress" in the NASV and "sport" in the KJV is "tsachaq" (Strong's number 6711). The same word is translated "laugh" in Genesis 18:13 to describe Sarah's reaction to the prophecy of her pregnancy and to describe Ishmael's mocking of Isaac in Genesis 21:9. The Strong's definition is "to laugh outright (in merriment or scorn) by implication to sport." Nowhere else is the word translated "caress." Isaac and Rebecca were not necessarily doing anything more than playing around, albeit in a way as to convince Abimelech that they were not merely brother and sister.*

4. What kind of man is Abimelech? What does he value?

5. Why does tension arise between the Philistines and Isaac and his family?

6. Why would wells be so important between the Philistines and Isaac's servants?

7. How does Isaac respond? What is the result?

8. What are the consequences for Isaac and Rebekah?

Lesson 19.
Jacob and Esau
Genesis 27

1. What does Isaac ask of Esau?

2. What does Rebekah tell Jacob to do?

3. Who did Isaac intend to bless? What did he ask from Esau?

4. What revenge did Esau vow?

5. What did Rebekah advise Jacob to do in order to save himself?

6. Why did Rebekah send Jacob to Laban (her brother)?

Background: *When teaching my children, I'm usually looking for examples of truthfulness, preferably truthfulness <u>rewarded</u>. So passages like this one make my feeble heart a little nervous. How will I answer the child who looks up at me and says, "But Mommy, he lied!" I'm forced to concede that sometimes things aren't easy. While I may not have the "fountain-of-all-wisdom" answer for my children, I can acknowledge that 1) Jacob and his mother did deceive Isaac (behavior I would punish); 2) God's will (Genesis 25:23) was accomplished none the less - In addition to receiving God's judgement, Esau lost what he had already despised; 3) There were consequences for Jacob's deceit — fear, further estrangement from his father and brother, and exile. Had Jacob and Rebekah appealed to God to intervene rather than resorting to deceit, perhaps we would have seen a different story. Because they didn't, we have another type of example for our children - one of how God works His will in spite of our petty fears and disobedience.*

Maps: *On map #3 in **The Student Bible Atlas,** you can trace the route Jacob took to visit his uncle Laban in Haran.*

Lesson 20.
Jacob's Ladder
Isaac sends Jacob to Laban
Genesis 28

1.   What blessing and command does Isaac make to Jacob?

2.   What is Esau's reaction to the departure of Jacob and his parents' concern that he not marry a Canaanite? What does his action reveal about his character?

3.   What does Jacob see in his dream?

4.   What promise does he hear?

5.   What promise does he make?

6.   Do you think Jacob's actions reveal a change in his character?

Lesson 21.
Jacob, Laban, Leah, & Rachel
Genesis 29-31

1.   Describe Jacob's arrival.

2.   What deal does Jacob make with Laban?

3.   How well does Laban keep his word? In what way is this a fitting experience for Jacob?

4.   Jacob and Leah have four sons, Rachel has no children — Why?

5.   Who gives children?

6.   List Jacob's children in order by mother.

7.   Describe Jacob's departure from Laban. Why does Laban have a hard time letting go?

Background: *A word to the fainthearted. Do we read this passage unedited to our first graders? Yes! The focus of the story is on the children born to Jacob's wives. A child who asks more technical questions is probably <u>ready</u> for more technical answers.*

Background: *What about mandrakes? In our own reading of this chapter, I have explained that Reuben found a plant that Leah and Rachel thought would help them have a baby. Go from there to verse 17 to see the real reason for Issachar's conception.*

Lesson 22.
Jacob returns to Esau
Genesis 32-33

1. Why was Jacob concerned about Esau?

2. What does Jacob ask God to do about Esau?

3. What new name does God give to Jacob?

4. Why does Jacob fear Esau? Is Esau coming to meet him alone?

5. Why is it ironic that Jacob (having prospered) now wishes to bless Esau by giving him a gift? How does this behavior contrast with Jacob's earlier treatment of Esau?

Lesson 23.
Dinah and her brothers' Revenge
Genesis 34

1. How did Shechem treat Dinah?

2. What was Jacob's first reaction to the news that his daughter had been defiled?

3. What solution does Shechem propose? How do Jacob and his sons react?

4. Why are Hamor and Shechem anxious to be circumcised and become one people with Jacob and his sons?

5. Discuss the revenge taken by Dinah's brothers. Were their actions justified or excessive?

6. What is Jacob's reaction to the actions of Simeon and Levi? What justification do they offer for their actions?

7. How many brothers does Dinah have? Who is her father? her uncle? her grandfathers? How many of her relatives took action to defend her honor?

Background: *This is another, shall we say, "challenging" chapter. Yet it explains why there was some tension between Israel and the neighboring peoples and why Israel is continually commanded to be rid of foreign gods.*

Lesson 24.
Jacob's New Name
Genesis 35

1. What significant thing had happened earlier at Bethel?

2. Why does he command his household to remove all the foreign gods? Who does his household now include?

3. What does God say to Jacob?

4. How did Rachel die?

Background: *"Ben-oni" means "son of my sorrow"; "Ben-jamin" means "son of my right hand." This may refer both to Jacob's esteem for Rachel as well as a prophetic hope for his newborn son.*

Background: *Verse 22, Reuben's sin, is not dealt with here, but is referred to later on in Genesis 49:4 as Jacob summons and prophesies over his sons. Though you might choose to skip over this verse, it does tell much about Reuben's character which comes into play in the story of Joseph. It is also an example of how the sins of the fathers (in this case — deceit) are often magnified in their children.*

5. Who buried Isaac?

Background: *Genesis 36 records the generations of Esau who takes his wives from among the Canaanites, Hittites, and Hivites. We suggest you read 36:1-8 and then move on to chapter 37.*

Lesson 25.
Joseph Betrayed by his Brothers
Genesis 37

Background: *Remember, Joseph is next to the youngest. He is 17, and all his older brothers are probably full-grown, and possibly married men.*

1. How does Jacob's treatment of Joseph differ from his treatment of his other sons?

2. What is the first account of Joseph we read? Do his actions endear him to his brothers?

3. What is the significance of Joseph's dream? How is it received? Why do you think the brothers respond the way they do? What is his father's response?

4. Should Joseph have told his dreams to his brothers? Why do you think his father rebuked him?

5. How did Reuben save Joseph's life?

   Remember, Reuben is the oldest of the brothers and also the son of Leah... Joseph is the son of Rachel...

6. Is Judah trying to save Joseph as well? Is his action better or worse than Reuben's? Why?

   Remember, Judah is the fourth (and youngest) of Leah's sons. Both he and Reuben are grown men here, probably in their late 20's or early 30's.

7. Did Reuben participate in the scheme to sell Joseph into slavery?

8. Did Reuben participate in the cover-up?

Thought: *If your brothers do something wrong, you share their guilt if you help to cover it up, even if you were not a participant.*

9. What happens to Joseph?

Lesson 26.
Judah and Tamar
Genesis 38

1. Where does Judah take a wife? How does this compare with the practice of Isaac and Jacob...

Background: *His first son was evil in the sight of the LORD, so the LORD took his life. His second son was supposed to help his first son's wife, but he was selfish. "And what he did was displeasing in the sight of the LORD; so he took his life also."*

Judah refuses to give his third son to Tamar as a new husband, and then after his wife dies, he refuses to help Tamar himself.

Verse nine is the most difficult verse for young audiences. You could summarize it this way if you wish, "Onan knew that any children he fathered wouldn't be his, so he selfishly and rudely refused to help."

2. How does Tamar trick Judah into lying with her?

3. Why does Judah not launch a search to find the woman he gave his seal, cord, and staff?

4. What is Judah's reaction when he realizes who has his things?

Background: *This is a puzzling story. Part of the lesson is certainly the example of Judah's two wicked sons who displeased God so much that he took their lives. I'm not quite sure what to make of Tamar's persistence in seeking to have an heir descended from Judah (this was what she had bargained for in marrying the oldest son of Judah) but her method hardly seems to be one that God could approve of. Nonetheless, from Judah and Tamar is continued the lineage of David and eventually the Messiah.*

There are enough troubling elements in this story that you may want to skip lightly over it. The details of how Onan shirked his responsibility to his dead older brother are probably not something you need to go into with younger children. But then again, they are very unlikely to ask, even if you read the chapter word for word. If they do ask, and are persistent, and are of a certain age (I am deliberately not committing myself to a specific number here) then you may have an opportunity to introduce certain facts to them. Be sensitive. Our own rule has been to answer honest questions as simply as possible when they come up, but not to attempt to provide more detail than is specifically asked for by the child. So far, this seems to have worked well.

Lesson 27.
Joseph in Potiphar's house
Genesis 39

"The LORD was with Joseph, so he became a successful man." **Genesis 39:2**

1. Who, according to Joseph, would he sin against by lying with Potiphar's wife?

2. How does Joseph respond to Potiphar's wife?

3. If God rewards those who do good, why does Joseph end up in prison?

4. Joseph was right, but was punished unjustly. How does he respond?

5. How does God show his love and care for Joseph?

Background: *I read this pretty much as is. I may add a little dialogue, like "Kiss me, Joseph" in a whining, obnoxious voice. The children understand that this is a wicked woman and that Joseph is right to flee. If any explanation is necessary, I have asked them, "How would you like it if I started treating someone other than your Dad like I was married to him?" They don't have to know explicit details in order to understand that Potiphar's wife is bad news.*

Lesson 28.
The Baker, the Cupbearer, and Joseph
Genesis 40

1. Joseph is unjustly imprisoned. Describe his attitude.

2. How does he respond to the other prisoners? What does this show about his character?

3. Who does Joseph say allows him to interpret the dreams?

4. Joseph has a wonderful opportunity to use his "connections" to bring his plight before the authorities and be released... but he isn't... why?

5. What happens to the Cupbearer and the Baker? Why isn't Joseph released when the cupbearer is restored to office? How much longer must Joseph remain in jail?

Hint: *God is allowing Joseph to remain in prison until the proper time — when he has big plans for Joseph... Not just freedom, but raising him up over all Egypt.*

Lesson 29.
Pharaoh's Bad Dream
Genesis 41

1. What did Pharaoh dream?

2. Why is Joseph called?

3. Who does Joseph say can interpret dreams? What does this show us about Joseph's character and his relationship with God?

4. How does Pharaoh respond to the interpretation?

    Joseph, 30 years old, goes from younger brother
    >to slave
    >to prisoner
    >to forgotten prisoner
    >to freedom
    >to being given complete authority over all Egypt

5. Describe Joseph's new life. What do his sons' names mean? What does this tell us about Joseph?

Background: *Joseph's wife, Asenath, was the daughter of Potiphera, priest of On. The city On was also known as Hieropolis. This city was the center of worship for the cult of Ra, god of the sun. The priests of On were the elite, thought to be the most learned of all Egyptians. Associated with the temple of Ra was a medical school and a training center for the priests of On.*

"And the people of all the earth came to Egypt to buy grain from Joseph..." **Genesis 41:57**

Lesson 30.
Joseph's brothers come to Egypt
Genesis 42

1. Why do Joseph's brothers come to Egypt?

2. Who does Jacob keep with him? Why?

3. Describe Joseph's meeting with his brothers. How does he react? How does he test them?

4. To what do the brothers attribute their troubles? What does this show us about them? What does it show Joseph? Why do you think he weeps?

5. Tell about the money in the grain sacks. How did it get there? Why?

6. What does Joseph demand of his brothers? What does Jacob say when he hears?

7. Why is Jacob so attached to Benjamin?

Lesson 31.
Joseph's brothers come back to Egypt
Genesis 43-44

Chapter 43

1. Which of the brothers is spokesman in dealing with Jacob about the return to Egypt? Is he the oldest?

2. What promise does Judah make to Jacob concerning Benjamin? Has his character changed since he proposed the sale of Joseph into slavery?

3. How do the brothers react to being brought to Joseph's house? What are they afraid of?

4. How is Joseph assured of his brothers' honesty?

5. Seeing Benjamin deeply moves Joseph. Why?

6. Why does Joseph eat separately from his brothers at the feast in his house?

Chapter 44

7. Describe the second trick with money and a silver cup in the grain bags. What is Joseph trying to do? Why? What happens?

8. Who speaks for the brothers to Joseph? Is he the oldest of the brothers?

9. What does Judah offer in order to appease Joseph?

Joseph reveals himself to his Brothers
Genesis 45-46:7

1. Why does Joseph clear the room?

2. Why are the brothers dismayed?

3. How does Joseph respond to his brothers? Does Joseph forgive his brothers? Does Joseph understand why he was sold into slavery? What does this tell us about the kind of person Joseph is?

Background: *Note that Joseph was so important and liked in Egypt that Pharaoh immediately extended an invitation to Joseph's father and brothers to move to Egypt and settle there.*

4. How did Jacob react to the news his sons brought him?

5. What does God tell Jacob he will do?

Background: *Genesis 46:8-27 lists all of Jacob's sons and grandchildren, cataloging who went into Egypt. Notice how many of Jacob's house made the journey and remember it. It will be useful to compare with the number who come out of Egypt in the Exodus.*

Lesson 33.
Jacob/Israel settles in Egypt — Goshen
Genesis 46:28-34 & 47

1. Who is leading all of Jacob/Israel's family?

2. Why did Joseph intend that his family give their occupation as "keepers of livestock?"

3. Why did he direct his family to Goshen?
   hint: see 47:6 — Pasture for livestock was the best land in Egypt

4. Why didn't he just give everyone the food that they asked for? How do the people respond to him?

5. What was the level of taxation in Egypt? What portion of GNP did Pharaoh take? Compare this with current levels of taxation in countries around the world... (Ah, for the good old days of Pharaoh!)

6. What three groups owned land in Egypt after the famine?

7. What is Israel/Jacob's final request of Joseph before he dies? Why?

Lesson 34.
Jacob's Blessing
Genesis 48-49

Background: *Jacob explicitly recognizes as his legitimate heirs, the two sons of Joseph born of an Egyptian princess in Egypt. Indeed, he says all their descendants will be known not by the name of the tribe of Joseph, but by the names of Ephraim and Manasseh (fruitful and forgetful)!*

Joseph's sons thus each get an equal share with their 11 uncles. Joseph by this reckoning has a double share.

From the tribe of Ephraim come both Joshua and Jeroboam, the conqueror of the promised land and the rebel who established the Northern Kingdom of the 10 tribes of Israel after Solomon's death.

"Judah — from you shall come the kings..."

Just read the blessing of Jacob. The poetic descriptions and prophecies about the tribes will evoke some echoes now... perhaps more later.

Lesson 35.

The death of Jacob/Israel and of Joseph
Genesis 50

1. How is Israel's body prepared for burial?

Background: *The Tomb of the Patriarchs is in Hebron, still there, still revered by both Jews and Moslems. Mohammed traced his people's lineage back to Ishmael and Abraham.*

2. Does Joseph have any trouble getting permission to depart from Egypt in order to bury his father? Remember this when a later request is made of another pharaoh...

3. What are Joseph's brothers worried about after Jacob's death? What do they do? How does Joseph respond? What does his response tell us about his character?

"And as for you, you meant evil against me, but God meant it for good in order to bring about this present result, to preserve many people alive." **Genesis 50:20**

Note: *verse 23 indicates that Joseph was a grandfather (Machir) and a great-grandfather (the sons of Machir) before he died.*

Joseph promises his brothers that God will surely take care of them and bring them up to the land promised to Abraham, Isaac, and Jacob. But it will not be in a peaceful, triumphal procession as it was when Jacob was buried... it will be more astounding and unusual than that. On to the Exodus...

Lesson 36.

Egypt forgets Joseph
Exodus 1

1. How many people came with Joseph's brothers to settle in Egypt?
2. What happened after Joseph and his brothers died?
3. What is the new Pharaoh worried about?
4. Does he remember what Joseph did for Egypt?
5. What command did the king of Egypt give to the Hebrew midwives? Did they obey?
6. What did they say when the king asked why they had disobeyed?
7. Did God punish them for lying?
8. How did God specifically reward the Hebrew midwives?
9. What command did Pharaoh give "all his people" concerning Hebrew children?

Lesson 37.
The Birth of Moses
Exodus 2

1. How old was Moses when his mother hid him in the basket at the river?

2. Was Moses' mother obeying Pharaoh by "casting Moses into the Nile?" In what way was she disobeying? Was she wrong to disobey? Would she have been wrong to obey? Why?

3. Who found Moses?

4. Why did she send the child back with a "nurse" from among the Hebrews?

5. Who named Moses? What relationship did he have with the Egyptian princess?

Background: *For more commentary on Moses' youth see also Acts 7:19-22 ("he was educated in all the learning of the Egyptians") and Hebrews 11:23-27 ("Moses refused to be called the son of Pharaoh's daughter").*

6. Did Moses share in the suffering of the Hebrew people?

7. How did he react when he went out and saw their hard labors? What did Pharaoh do? What did Moses do? Use a map to locate the place Moses went to.

8. How did Moses react to the mistreatment of the priest of Midian's daughters? Do you begin to see a pattern to his life & reactions?

9. What is God's reaction to the sighs, cries, and groaning of the sons of Israel?

<h1 align="center">Lesson 38.</h1>

Moses and the Burning Bush
Exodus 3 & 4:1-17

Background: *Find Horeb on a map. It is also called mount Sinai and in this passage, the mountain of God. It is the location of both the Burning Bush and later, the giving of the Ten Commandments.*

Chapter 3

1. What was Moses' occupation in Midian?

2. What was Moses' reaction to the sight of the burning bush?

3. What is Moses first reaction when The Voice identifies itself?

4. What does God reveal to Moses about what he is about to do?

5. What objection does Moses make about going to Pharaoh? How does God answer?

6. What objection does Moses make about going to the sons of Israel? How does God answer?

7. Does God expect Pharaoh to say yes to Moses' request?

8. What does God say the women of Israel will take with them into the wilderness?

Chapter 4

9. What objection does Moses make the third time?

10. What three signs does God give?

11. What objection does Moses make the fourth time? How does God answer?

12. What objection does Moses make the fifth time? How does God react?

Suggestion: *The five exchanges between God and Moses become clearer if you chart them. Draw a line down the middle of a sheet of paper and write at the top of the left column, "Moses' objections" and at the top of the right column "God's answers."*

Lesson 39.
Moses returns to Egypt
Exodus 4:18-31 & 5

Chapter 4:18-31

1. What does God say to Moses about what to expect from Pharaoh?

2. What prophecy about his son is Moses directed to deliver to Pharaoh?

3. Did the people question the message from Moses and Aaron?

4. What did they do when they heard that God was concerned for them?

Background: *Verses 24-26 relates briefly God's threatening the life of Moses, because he has not circumcised his son, i.e. he has not had him marked with the sign of the covenant. This may have been a lesson to remind Moses that it is God's wrath which is to be feared, not Pharaoh and that God's ordinances are to be taken seriously (cf. Genesis 17:14). It is also a sign that God has provided the means by which to turn aside his wrath, involving blood and the sign of the covenant... elements which are to be repeated in the Passover that culminates in the deliverance of Israel from Egypt.*

Chapter 5

5. In whose name does Moses make his request of Pharaoh?

6. What is Pharaoh's reaction to Moses? What does Pharaoh say about his relationship to the LORD?

7. What command does Pharaoh give Moses and Aaron? What command does he give to the taskmasters and the foreman?

8. What does Pharaoh say is the real reason why Israel wishes to go into the wilderness to worship the LORD?

9. What change has Moses brought about for the people of Israel? Are they grateful?

10. What does Moses say to God?

Lesson 40.
God's Promise to Moses
Exodus 6:1-13 & 6:28 –7:25

1. How does God identify himself to Moses?

2. What does God tell Moses to say to the sons of Israel?

I am the LORD
I will bring you out
I will deliver you
I will also redeem you
I will take you for MY people
I will be your God
I will bring you to the land
I will give it to you for a possession
I am the LORD

3. How do the sons of Israel respond? Why?

4. What objection does Moses make about going back to Pharaoh?

5. To whom is God going to demonstrate that he is the LORD?

The First Plague: The Nile turned to Blood

Background: *In the first plague Moses strikes the Nile with his staff and it is turned to blood. The Nile was worshipped as a god by the Egyptians. They referred to the Nile as "the source of life." Another name for Egypt was "the gift of the Nile."*

6. When God turns the Nile to blood, what is he trying to show Pharaoh and the Egyptians about the true source of life?

God's Promise to Moses
Exodus 6:1-13 & 6:28 –7:25
(continued)

Background: *As you start the section on the plagues, you may want to keep a chart with your children summarizing some of the important details about the ten plagues. Pharaoh's reaction to each one is an obvious detail to note, but so is the reaction of Pharaoh's magicians and for the later plagues, Pharaoh's servants. It is also interesting to note the effect of the plagues on the Hebrews in Goshen.*

Sign/Plague	Magicians	Pharaoh's Servants	Pharaoh's Reaction	Effect on Israel
0. Staff/Serpent	duplicate		did not listen	
1. Blood	duplicate		did not listen	
2. Frogs	duplicate		I will let you go!	
3. Gnats	could NOT duplicate		did not listen	
4. Flies	??		I will let you go!	Goshen set apart
5. Livestock	??		did not listen	unaffected
6. Boils	afflicted!		did not listen	??
7. Hail		some feared/were spared	I will let you go!	unaffected
8. Locusts		Let the men GO!	The men may go!	??
9. Darkness			The people — but not the flocks — may go.	unaffected
10. Firstborn		Send them out in haste!	Everybody GO!	unaffected

We have used the following rhyme as we've studied the plagues to help us keep them
straight:
Blood, frogs, gnats and flies
Cattle died
Boils, hail, locusts, dark
Egypt wails, all depart.

Lesson 41.
Frogs and Gnats
Exodus 8

The Second Plague: Frogs

Background: *The second plague is an overabundance of frogs. One of the gods worshiped by the Egyptians was Hequet, whose image was a woman with the head of a frog. Hequet was the goddess of birth, midwives, and safe deliveries.*

1. How extensive was the plague of frogs? In what kinds of places did the Egyptians find frogs?

2. How enthusiastically would the Egyptians have worshiped Hequet that week?

3. What is Pharaoh's reaction? What does he ask Moses to do? What does he promise Moses he will do?

4. Compare his attitude now with that during the first plague... (cf. 7:23)

5. How did Pharaoh react after Moses and Aaron ended the plague of frogs?

The Third Plague: Gnats

6. Pharaoh's magicians had been able to duplicate the first and second plagues, but they are unsuccessful with the third. What is their reaction to this? What is Pharaoh's response?

The Fourth Plague: Flies

7. A new detail is introduced with the fourth plague. God protects Goshen and the Hebrews from the swarms of insects? Why does God say he is doing this?

8. What is Pharaoh's response to the fourth plague?

9. What does Pharaoh do after God ended the fourth plague?

Lesson 42.
Cattle died, Boils, Hail
Exodus 9

The Fifth Plague: Livestock Die

1. Did Pharaoh know that God spared the livestock of the Hebrews? How? What was his reaction?

The Sixth Plague: Boils

2. What specific group of Egyptians are reported to have been afflicted with boils? Why is their mention significant?

The Seventh Plague: Hail

3. God tells Moses to warn Pharaoh about the coming plague of hail. How did the servants of Pharaoh respond to the warning? What happened to the livestock of those who "paid no regard to the word of the LORD?"

4. What is Pharaoh's response to the plague of hail?

5. What does Moses say about the repentance of Pharaoh?

6. What does Pharaoh do after the thunder and hail ceased?

Lesson 43.
Locusts and Darkness
Exodus 10 & 11

Chapter 10
The Eighth Plague: Locusts

1. Moses again warns Pharaoh of the coming plague. What is the reaction of Pharaoh's servants?

2. What compromise does Pharaoh offer? What is Moses' response?

3. What is Pharaoh's response after the plague of locusts starts?

4. What is Pharaoh's response after the plague of locusts ends?

The Ninth Plague: Darkness

5. Exodus describes the darkness as "even a darkness which may be felt." How dark do you think this was?

6. What compromise does Pharaoh offer now? What is Moses' response?

Chapter 11

Background: *This chapter is a pause and summary between the first 9 plagues and the 10th plague - the death of the firstborn.*

7. In spite of the plagues which have afflicted Egypt, how do the Egyptian people feel about the Hebrews? How do they regard Moses?

8. Moses warns Pharaoh about the coming plague — "all the firstborn in the land of Egypt shall die." What is Pharaoh's response?

Lesson 44.
Preparations for the Passover
Exodus 12

1. Who does God command to celebrate the Passover? Who is commanded to take a lamb?

2. What sign is to be made to mark houses where the Passover has been celebrated?

3. In Exodus 12:12, God explains why he will go through Egypt and slay the firstborn. Who is he judging?

4. Moses gives two commands concerning Passover. The ceremonies are to preserve the Hebrews from the angel of death, but they are also to be repeated each year AFTER they enter the promised land... why?

5. What is Pharaoh's reaction to the death of the firstborn? Does he wait until the next morning to speak to Moses? Why?

Lesson 45.
Israel leaves Egypt
Exodus 13

1. What command does God give Moses concerning the firstborn?

2. Why is Israel instructed to keep the Passover feast?

3. God did not take Israel to the promised land by the most direct route, why?

4. Why did Moses take the bones of Joseph with him?

5. How did God guide Israel?

Lesson 46.
The Parting of the Red Sea
Exodus 14 & 15

Chapter 14

1. Why did Pharaoh pursue Israel? What does this tell us about Pharaoh's character?

2. What did God say he would bring about for Pharaoh, his army, and the Egyptians?

3. How does Israel react when they see Pharaoh and his army approaching? How does Moses answer them?

   the pillar of cloud moved between Egypt & Israel

   The LORD swept the sea back by a strong east wind all night

   The LORD looked down... and brought the army of the Egyptians into confusion

   ... and the sea returned to its normal state at daybreak

Chapter 15

This chapter contains the song of Moses in celebration of the victory over Pharaoh and his army.

Maps: *Map # 4 in **The Student Bible Atlas** shows the route of the Exodus.*

Lesson 47.
Quail, Manna, Water, and Victory
Exodus 16 & 17

This lesson could be subtitled, "So what have you done for us lately?"

Chapter 16

1. How long have the Hebrews been out of Egypt? How would you describe them?

2. Were the Hebrews grateful for their deliverance from Egypt?

3. What did God send for the Hebrews to eat?

4. What happened when they gathered too much and tried to hoard the manna? What application can we draw from this?

Chapter 17

5. What do we find the Hebrews doing at the beginning of chapter 17?

6. After God has fed Israel with quail and manna, are they satisfied?

7. How do they react to the water shortage? Do they trust Moses? Do they trust God?

Note: *This is the first mention of Joshua.*

8. What is the relationship between Moses and the tide of battle?

9. How is Moses able to keep his hands up so that Israel will prevail? What application does this have for us today?

Lesson 48.
Moses and Jethro
Exodus 18

1. How does Jethro respond to the news of the deliverance from Egypt?
2. What is Jethro's concern about Moses' duties as judge over Israel?
3. What suggestion does he make to Moses?
4. How does Moses respond to Jethro's advice?
5. What cases were reserved for Moses to decide?
6. What were the qualifications for the judges that Moses chose?

Lesson 49.
God's Covenant with Israel
Exodus 19 & 20

Chapter 19

1. God reminds Israel of what he has done... what were they? List the things he says to Moses.
2. God promises Israel what he will do... List the promises.
3. What does God ask Israel to do?
4. What does Israel promise to Moses?
5. What signs were there that God had descended on Mt. Sinai?
   thunder and lightning
   thick cloud
   a very loud trumpet sound
   smoke
   the mountain quaked violently

Chapter 20

This chapter tells the story of God giving the law to Israel

Background: *God's deliverance of Israel from bondage in Egypt and the dramatic signs of his presence on the mountain were intended to emphasize the divine origin of the commandments and to emphasize their importance. Play up the drama of the situation with your listeners.*

6. What is the first commandment?
   Actually, they are all worth memorizing. And all children used to be required to memorize them as a part of their catechism.

Lesson 50.
Aaron and the Golden Calf
Exodus 32

Egypt forgot Joseph and now Israel has forgotten Moses... How long did it take?

1. What do the people ask Aaron? Notice who they say brought them out of Egypt.

2. How does Aaron respond? How should he have responded? Does Aaron attempt to turn Israel back towards God? What does Aaron do?

3. Did Joshua participate in the idolatry?

4. Describe God's conversation with Moses over the activity in the camp.

5. What did Moses do to the stone tablets with the law on them? Why?

6. What is Aaron's explanation of his actions? According to Aaron, how did the calf come to be? Does he admit making the calf?

7. What is the consequence of the people's idolatry? How many died?

8. How does Moses attempt to atone for the people's sin? What is God's response?

Lesson 51.
Moses Gets New Tablets
Exodus 33-34

Chapter 33

1. God announces that he will not go up in Israel's midst...
   What is Israel's reaction?

2. What was the purpose of the "tent of meeting?" Who would meet there? Why?

3. What do we know about Joshua so far? What is important to him?

4. Describe Moses' relationship with God.

5. What does Moses ask of God?

6. What does God mean when he says "no man can see me and live?"

Chapter 34

7. How does the LORD reveal himself in 34:6-7? Why does he do this?

8. How does Moses respond?

9. Describe the covenant. What warning and command does God give Israel to remember when they enter the promised land?

10. What is different about Moses when he returns with the law from Mount Sinai?

11. How did Aaron and Israel react to Moses' appearance?

Background: *Exodus 35-40 describes the construction of the tabernacle. How much of it you'll want to read aloud will depend on the age and attention span of your children. You may want to read it all and make a model of the tabernacle as you read. Or you may want to summarize and move on to Numbers.*

Lesson 52.
Grumbling, Complaining, and Rebellion
Numbers 11 & 12

Background: *The book of Numbers begins with a census of "all the congregation of the sons of Israel," a recap of various laws and ordinances (paralleled in Exodus and Deuteronomy) and preparations to "set out to the place the Lord had promised them" (Numbers 10:29-30).*

Chapter 11

1. How are the people described in Numbers 11:1 and what does the LORD do? Why is God angry with Israel?

2. What are the "rabble's" specific complaints?

3. Describe Moses prayer in Numbers 11:11-23. Why is Moses angry? What does Moses ask God to do? How does the Lord respond to Moses?

4. How does God provide meat for all of Israel? What happens to the greedy?

Chapter 12

5. Why do Miriam and Aaron speak against Moses? How does God respond to this sibling rivalry? (Hint: There are some family applications possible here.)

6. What does God say to Miriam and Aaron about Moses?

7. What is the consequence of Miriam's rebellion?

8. How is Miriam healed and restored?

Lesson 53.
Spies into Canaan
Numbers 13 & 14

Chapter 13

1. Why does Moses send out spies? Who is sent?

2. How do the spies describe the land?

3. What do the spies recommend that Israel do?

4. What is Caleb's opinion?

Chapter 14

5. What does Israel want to do?

6. What do Caleb and Joshua do?

7. Describe Moses' conversation with God in verses 11-30. Compare verse 18 with Exodus 34:6-7.

8. What is the consequence of the people's lack of faith?

9. What happened to the spies who brought the bad report?

10. What further rebellion and disobedience does Israel attempt? What happens as a consequence?

Lesson 54.
The Rebellion of Korah
Numbers 16

1. How many rebel with Korah? What do they accuse Moses of?

2. What do Dathan and Abiram accuse Moses of?

3. How do they describe Egypt? How accurate are their memories of Egypt?

4. What does God say to Moses and Aaron?

5. What happens to Korah, Dathan, and Abiram?

6. What does God direct Eleazar to do with the censers of the men whom the LORD consumed?

7. Initially, what is the reaction of Israel to God's judgement on Korah, et al? How do they respond the next day? What happens to Israel as a result?

Lesson 55.
Serpents among the People
Numbers 20 - 21:9

Chapter 20

1. What is Israel's complaint this time?

2. How does God provide water for Israel? Why was the place call the waters of Miribah?

Background: *Verse 14. Do you remember who the ancestor of Edom is? (Esau, Jacob / Israel's brother).*

3. How does Edom respond to Israel's request?

4. Tell about Aaron's death. Why isn't he allowed to enter the land?

Chapter 21

5. Who attacked Israel? What happened?

6. What is Israel's complaint now? *(This is getting kind of repetitive, isn't it?)*

7. What was the consequence of Israel's complaint?

8. What are God's instructions to Moses about how to deal with the serpents?

Background: *Read to your children John 3:14 - this is background to John 3:16...*

Remember to follow the journey of Israel through the wilderness on a map.

Lesson 56.

Balaam and Balak
Numbers 22-24

Chapter 22

1. Do you remember who Moab is? What is the origin of his family?
2. What does Balak fear?
3. What does he ask Balaam to do?
4. What does the LORD tell Balaam to do?
5. Is Balaam a prophet? Is he of the house of Israel?
6. How does Balak try to persuade Balaam to come?
7. Describe Balaam's donkey ride. Does anything unusual happen?
8. What was Balaam's reaction when he saw the angel of the LORD?

Chapter 23

9. What does Balaam do when he surveys Israel camped on the edge of Moab?
10. Describe Balak's repeated attempts to make Balaam curse Israel. How does Balaam respond each time?
11. What kind of prophecy does Balak finally get?

Background: *Balaam's two prophetic utterances in Numbers 24 have a double fulfillment. First, when the kingdom of Israel is established and does establish rule over the existing nations of Canaan. It is also understood to be a prophecy of the Messiah ("a star shall come forth from Jacob, and a scepter shall rise from Israel").*

Lesson 57.

Israel plays the Harlot
Numbers 25

After Balaam has reminded Balak of what God has done to deliver Israel from Egypt, now Israel demonstrates that she has forgotten what Balaam remembers.

1. What do the people of Israel do with the daughters of Moab?
2. What does God command Moses to do in judgement?
3. What does Phineas do? What effect does this action have on the plague?
4. What does God say about what Phineas did?
5. How seriously does God take Israel's sin here? What should we learn about God's character?

Lesson 58.
Israel defeats Two Kings
Deuteronomy 1-3

Chapter 1

1. When Deuteronomy opens, how long have the people been wandering in the wilderness? Where are they?

2. Moses reminds Israel what God had said at Mount Horeb. What had God said?

3. Moses reminds Israel of their rebellion and grumbling in the episode of the spies. Why?

4. Moses reminds Israel of God's judgement about who would enter the promised land. Who did God say he would allow? Who will he not allow? Why?

Chapter 2

5. What nations does Moses remind Israel that God has told them not to fight? Why?

6. What king and nation does Israel contend with first?

7. What reputation does God say he will give Israel among the nations?

Chapter 3

8. What king and nation does Israel contend with now?

9. What example does Moses say he has set for Joshua? How is Israel to behave when she crosses the Jordan? When are the men of Israel told they can rest and return to their families and cities?

10. What request does Moses make of God? Why is it rejected? What does God command Moses to do?

Lesson 59.

Moses teaches Israel the Law
Deuteronomy 4-5

Chapter 4

1. Why does Moses repeat the statutes and judgments?

2. Who is he talking to? Haven't they heard them all before?

3. What does Moses say will happen to Israel if they turn aside to idolatry?

Chapter 5

4. Why does Moses repeat the ten commandments?

Lesson 60.

Moses commands Israel
Deuteronomy 6-7

Chapter 6

1. As Moses is teaching Israel the law, what does he command the fathers whom he is teaching to do?

2. What does Moses promise God will do if the fathers of Israel are faithful to teach their sons?

Chapter 7

3. What command does God give Israel concerning their relations with the seven nations of Canaan?

4. What does God say the consequence of disobedience will be?

5. What does God say the blessings for obedience will be?

6. What does God say will happen to the nations of Canaan?

Lesson 61.
Why God will give Israel Victory
Deuteronomy 8-9

Chapter 8

1. Why does Moses remind Israel of how God cared for them during the hardships of the wilderness?

2. What does he fear that Israel will do when they settle in the promised land and become prosperous?

Chapter 9

3. What error does Moses warn may arise from Israel's military victories?

4. Why does God say he is driving out the nations of Canaan before Israel?

5. Has God chosen Israel because of their righteousness? Is God giving them victory because of their righteous behavior in the wilderness?

6. What characteristics has Israel displayed in the wilderness?

Lesson 62.
Moses commands Israel
Deuteronomy 10-11

Chapter 10

1. What does Moses exhort Israel to remember and do?

2. What characteristics of God does Moses emphasize?

3. What does Moses remind Israel that God has done to fulfill the promise to Abraham?

Chapter 11

4. How does Moses direct that the sons of Israel (as yet unborn) shall know about the things God has done?

Moses commands Israel
Deuteronomy 12-13

Chapter 12

1. What is God's command concerning the gods of the nations of Canaan?

Chapter 13

2. What is to be done with a prophet or dreamer who entices you towards idolatry?
3. What is to be done with a relative who entices you towards idolatry?
4. What is to be done with a city which turns to idolatry?
5. How seriously does God take the sin of idolatry?

Moses commands Israel
Deuteronomy 14-16

Chapter 14

1. Why does God command Israel not to eat any detestable thing?
2. What items are to be tithed? What is Israel commanded to do with the tithe?

Chapter 15

3. What is to happen to debts every seven years?
4. What does God say about the tendency not to make loans in the sixth year?
5. How long may one keep a Hebrew slave?
6. How is a slave to be treated when he is freed?

Chapter 16

7. Why are the festivals of Passover, Weeks, and Booths to be celebrated?

*Consider celebrating Passover, or one of the other feasts, as a family. A good reference to help you with this is **Celebrate the Feasts**, by Zimmerman.*

Lesson 65.
The King, Priests, Prophets, and Detestable Practices
Deuteronomy 17-18

Chapter 17

1. What is to be done with someone who serves other gods and worships them?

2. What are the people to do with difficult legal cases?

3. What are God's qualifications for a king? What is he commanded not to do? What is he commanded to do?

4. What is to be the king's attitude towards God's law?

Note: *Remember these instructions. They will be a useful standard to refer back to when we come to the period of the kings.*

Chapter 18

5. How are the Levites to be fed and housed?

6. What are the "detestable practices" of the nations of Canaan?

7. Why is God driving out the nations of Canaan?

8. What is Israel's attitude towards these "detestable practices" supposed to be?

9. How is Israel to treat the prophet whom God will raise up?

10. How is Israel to treat one who presumptuously claims to be a prophet?

11. What is the test of a true prophet?

Lesson 66.
Blessings and Curses
Deuteronomy 29-30

Chapter 29

1. Where is Israel when this covenant is completed?

2. Who does God make the covenant with?

3. What does God say will happen if Israel turns aside to idolatry?

Chapter 30

4. What does God promise Israel if she repents after being exiled?

5. What choice does Moses set before Israel?

Lesson 67.
Moses' last Message
Deuteronomy 31-33

1. What prophecy does Moses make to Israel?

2. What does Moses say about himself?

3. Who does Moses say will cross the Jordan ahead of the people?

4. When the LORD meets Moses and Joshua at the door of the tent of meeting, what does He say about the people? Why are the people told to learn Moses' song?

5. What does Moses do with the Book of the Law?

Background: *Where does it say that Moses wrote the Pentateuch? Deuteronomy 31:24.*

Moses blessings on the twelve tribes are worth reading slowly aloud.

Lesson 68.
Moses and Joshua
Deuteronomy 34 & Joshua 1

Deuteronomy 34

1. Describe the death and burial of Moses. Where is Israel when Moses dies?
2. What has Joshua received from Moses?

Joshua 1

3. Why does God have to tell Joshua that Moses has died?
4. What does God specifically remind Joshua that he is to do as he leads Israel?
5. What is his confidence to be based on?
6. Why do you think the phrase "Be strong and courageous" is repeated 4 times?
7. How do the people respond to Joshua? (Get this in writing, Joshua!)
8. What commands does Joshua give the people?

Lesson 69.
Spies sent to Jericho
Joshua 2 & 3

Chapter 2

1. Does Rahab tell the truth about the spies? Was it wrong for her to lie?
2. What does Rahab know about Israel and about God?
3. What promise does Rahab ask the men of Israel to give her? Why?
4. What promise do the spies make to Rahab?
5. What report do the spies bring to Joshua?

Chapter 3

6. Why does Joshua direct the ark to lead the way?
7. What does Joshua tell the people to expect?
8. What does God say to Joshua that he will now begin to do?
9. What happens when the ark comes to the Jordan river?

Lesson 70.
Crossing the Jordan
Joshua 4 & 5

Chapter 4

1. Why does God command Joshua to take 12 stones from the Jordan?

2. How does Israel regard Joshua after the parting of the Jordan?

Chapter 5

3. What effect does the parting of the Jordan have on Israel's enemies?

4. Why does Israel need to be circumcised at Gilgal? What does this imply about their parents?

5. What would Israel have done in observing the Passover?

6. Why does the Manna cease?

7. Who is the man with a sword who appears to Joshua?

Maps: *Map #6 of **The Student Bible Atlas** shows the route of Joshua and Israel as they crossed the Jordan, attacked Jericho and Ai, and then campaigned to conquer the land of Canaan.*

Lesson 71.
Jericho and Ai
Joshua 6 & 7

Background: *This is a great story for your children to act out. We took all of the cushions off of our sofa and built the walls of Jericho. One child stood inside the walls and portrayed Rahab while all the others marched around seven times, and blew trumpets before watching the "walls" fall down. It's great fun! Though you might have to threaten to stone anyone who builds Jericho again without special permission!*

Chapter 6

1.   What do you suppose the people in Jericho thought as Israel marched around the walls each day for six days... but did not attack?

2.   What happens to Rahab? What happens to her family?

Background: *Now that Israel has won its first victory in the promised land over the Jordan, this is a good opportunity to review the summary of what God has done. Hebrews 11:1-31 gives a summary from Adam through Noah, Abraham, Isaac, Jacob, Joseph, Moses, and RAHAB! Isn't it interesting that she is mentioned, but not Joshua... why do you think this is? See Matthew 1:5 to see how Rahab fits into the lineage of Jesus.*

Chapter 7

3.   Why does Joshua send only a small force to take Ai?

4.   What happens when the army reaches Ai?

5.   How does Joshua react to the defeat? How does God answer him?

6.   Why does God say Israel was defeated?

Background: *There is a spiritual principle here, i.e. that if God's people have serious unconfessed, uncorrected sin among them, they are unable to stand before their enemies.*

7.   What has Achan done? What happens to him?

Background: *No, I don't have a definitive answer for why Achan's family and livestock perished with him. But it does seem that the effects of sin always reach farther than we ever intend.*

Lesson 72.
Joshua conquers Ai
Joshua 8 & Deuteronomy 7

1. As God sends Joshua against Ai a second time, what does he tell him?

2. What strategy does Joshua plan for his second assault on Ai?

3. What do Joshua and Israel do to the city of Ai and its inhabitants? Why?

Background: *The answer to why God commanded Israel to destroy Jericho and Ai so utterly is not immediately apparent in the book of Joshua. However, return to Deuteronomy 7 and you will see clearly the reasons why the nations of Canaan are being judged by God.*

4. Why is Israel commanded NOT to intermarry with the peoples of Canaan? *(see Deuteronomy, verses 4, 16, 25, 26)*

5. After Ai is destroyed, what does Joshua read to Israel? Why do you think he does this?

6. Why does God say he chose Israel?

7. Why does God tell Israel not to fear the seven nations?

8. Why does God command Israel to destroy the gods and idols of the seven nations?

Lesson 73.
Tricked by the Gibeonites
Joshua 9 & 10

Chapter 9

1. How do the Gibeonites convince Joshua and Israel that they have come from far away?

2. What did Joshua and Israel fail to do that would have uncovered the deception?

3. What promise/curse does Joshua make to the Gibeonites?

Chapter 10

4. Compare the attitude of Rahab, the Gibeonites, and the five kings toward Israel and its God.

5. In what way does God directly intervene to defeat the armies of the five kings?

    "There were more who died from the hailstones than those whom the sons of Israel killed with the sword." Joshua 10:11

Background: *Joshua's execution of the five kings may seem bloodthirsty, but remember 1) Instead of following the example of the Gibeonites who humbled themselves before Israel, these kings had allied themselves against Israel and attacked first... 2) God had commanded Israel to utterly destroy the seven nations because of their idolatry and wickedness...*
Makkedah
Libnah
Lachish
Gezer
Eglon
Hebron
Debir

These are the cities which Joshua destroyed... in fulfillment of God's direct command in Joshua 10:40.

Lesson 74.
Joshua's Final Battles
Joshua 11, 23, 24

"Just as the LORD had commanded Moses his servant, so Moses commanded Joshua, and so Joshua did; he left nothing undone of all that the LORD had commanded Moses." **Joshua 11:15**

This is the theme verse for the whole book of Joshua...

Background: *Many of the remaining chapters in Joshua might prove to be difficult read-alouds. You might try just reading enough to give your children a sense of what they include and then summarize when necessary. Chapter 12 lists kings conquered by Joshua. Chapters 13-22 details the division of the land among the twelve tribes of Israel. This is the ideal time to do a map of Israel showing the areas given to each of the twelve tribes.*

Chapter 23

1. What does Joshua remind the elders of? What acts of God does he recall?

2. What does he then command them to do?

3. Why does he say it is important to not turn aside?

4. What does Joshua say will happen if Israel forgets and begins to intermarry with the Canaanites?

Chapter 24

5. Both Joshua and Moses address the nation of Israel shortly before their deaths. Both recall the ways in which they had seen God working. Why was this an important thing to do? What application is there in this for our own lives?

"But as for me and my house, we will serve the LORD." **Joshua 24:15**

Lesson 75.
Unfinished Business
Judges 1-2

Chapter 1

1. Why do you think Judah is selected first to go up against the Canaanites?

2. Who leads Judah? What do they accomplish?

3. There is a repeated phrase in the rest of the chapter which sets the scene for the rest of the book of Judges, "but the sons of X did not drive out... " (Judah – v. 19; Benjamin – v.21; Manasseh – v.27; Ephraim – v. 29; Zebulun – v. 30; Asher – v. 31; Naphtali – v. 33)
Whom does each tribe fail to drive out?

Chapter 2

4. What part of the covenant has Israel failed to keep?

Background: *Verse 10 begins, "There arose a generation who did not know the LORD." Compare this with the earlier incident with "a Pharaoh who did not know Joseph."*

5. What was the institution of Passover supposed to remind the people of (and give fathers an opportunity to teach their children)?

6. Could this have happened if Israel had been celebrating Passover as commanded?

7. First Israel failed to drive out the Canaanites. Then they failed to teach their children. What happens next?

Background: *Verses 11-13 are among the most tragic in scripture... almost a second Fall!*

8. What is God's response to Israel's disobedience?

9. After they are chastised, how does God deliver them?

10. How does Israel react to the Judges whom God sent?

11. What course does God take when Israel's stubbornness in sin becomes apparent?

Lesson 76.

The First Judges: Othniel and Ehud

Judges 3

1. Why does the LORD leave the nations of Canaan in the midst of Israel?

2. How well does Israel obey the commandments of the LORD?

3. What specific sins does Israel commit while living among the Canaanites?

4. What does God do to discipline Israel?

5. What does God do to deliver Israel?

6. What happens after Othniel dies?

Background: *The next judge is someone to comfort your left-handed children with, Ehud - see verse 15.*

7. How does Ehud deliver Israel from Eglon, king of Moab?

8. How long does Israel have peace after Moab was subdued?

Lesson 77.

Deborah and Barak

Judges 4-5

Chapter 4

1. In addition to being a judge, what is Deborah?

2. Is she married?

3. Whom does Deborah summon to lead Israel in battle? What response does she get?

4. What does Heber the Kenite do?

5. What does Heber's wife, Jael do to Sisera?

Chapter 5: Deborah and Barak's song

6. What do Deborah and Barak give thanks for first?

7. How long is the land peaceful?
   "...and the land was undisturbed for 40 years!" Judges 5:31

Lesson 78.
Gideon, called to deliver Israel
Judges 6

1. Who now begins to oppress Israel?

Background: *A wine press is a circular tank-like structure with walls about 4-6 feet high to hold the grapes. Gideon is using it to hide his threshing of some small amount of wheat, probably with his staff. His choice of location implies that he is afraid of being observed or discovered. The angel's greeting may contain a healthy dose of sarcasm, e.g. Gideon isn't really a "valiant warrior," but rather a fearful farmer! Gideon's response to the call upon him delivered by the angel confirms this interpretation.*

2. What objection to the angel's announcement that "The Lord is with you" does Gideon make?

3. Is Gideon immediately obedient to the LORD's directive?

4. How does Gideon describe himself?

5. What specific action does God direct Gideon to do first?

6. Why does he do it by night?

7. Which of the tribes does Gideon summon? How does he do it?

8. What sign does Gideon ask of God to confirm that God has chosen him to deliver Israel?

9. Why do you think Gideon asked God to repeat the sign?

10. How would you describe Gideon's character?

11. What do we learn about God's character from his dealings with Gideon?

Lesson 79.
Gideon and his band of 300 Warriors
Judges 7-8

<u>Chapter 7</u>

1. How does the LORD tell Gideon to prepare for battle? Why does God say there are too many warriors?

2. How many does Gideon start out with? How many does he end up with?

3. How many men do the Midianites have?

4. Why does God tell Gideon to visit the Midianite camp with his servant?

5. What does Gideon hear?

6. How does Gideon win the battle?

<u>Chapter 8</u>

7. What is the response of the cities of Succoth and Penuel when Gideon asks for supplies for his men?

8. What does Gideon do to the cities after he returns from defeating Zebah and Zalmunna?

9. What do the people of Israel ask Gideon (and his son) to do after he executes Zebah and Zalmunna? What is Gideon's response?

10. What happens in Israel after Gideon's death?

Lesson 80.
Abimelech
Judges 9

1. What is Jerubbaal's other name?

2. What plot does Abimelech undertake in order to secure authority for himself alone?

3. Gideon had declined the offer to be Israel's king...why does Abimelech seek it?

4. What do the men of Shechem do to help Abimelech become king?

5. What does Joatham prophesy will happen to Abimelech and the men of Shechem?

6. What does Abimelech do to the city of Shechem after he has captured it?

7. What does Abimelech do the people who took refuge in the temple of El-berth?

8. What happens to Abimelech when he captured the city of Thebez?

Lesson 81.
Israel's pattern of Forgetfulness Jephthah
Judges 10 & 11

Chapter 10

1. How long is Israel at peace? Why does the peace end?

2. What other gods does Israel begin serving?

3. How many times has God delivered Israel now?

4. How does God answer their cries this time?

Chapter 11

5. Who are the Gileadites?

6. Why do Jephthah's half-brothers drive him out?

7. What bargain does Jephthah strike with the elders of Gilead in order to fight for them?

8. How much of Israel's history does Jephthah know? review: Who are Moab and Ammon? (Lot's sons!)

9. What vow does Jephthah make as he moves to make war on Ammon?

10. What must Jephthah do in order to fulfill his vow?

Background: *Jephthah's vow is the best known example of "rash promises." There are two interpretations for how he fulfilled his vow. One is that he sacrificed his daughter by putting her to death. The other is that he had her "set apart" and devoted as a perpetual virgin to service in some shrine or place of worship. Although human sacrifice was strictly forbidden to Israel, Jephthah is half-Canaanite and it is possible that he followed the tradition of the Canaanites. The author of Judges reports his actions without necessarily approving of them.*

11. Was Jephthah a man of God? before you decide, see 1 Samuel 12:11 where Samuel reminds Israel of all God has done and names Jephthah as one of the deliverers whom God sent...

Lesson 82.
Jephthah and Manoah
Judges 12 & 13

Chapter 12

1. Who threatens Jephthah and how is it resolved?

2. What judges succeed Jephthah and how long does each judge?

Chapter 13

3. What does Israel do (AGAIN!)? And here we go again... How does Israel do this time?

4. How does God judge Israel this time? With who? How long?

5. What specific instructions does the angel give to Samson's mother?

Background: Samson's "set-apartness" begins before he is born, and is important even though he is still in his mother's womb. You might make the obvious applications concerning the way God values people <u>before</u> they are born.

6. What is Manoah's response to the news from his wife?

7. What concern does Manoah have for his son (even before he is born!)?

8. How does Manoah respond to their meeting with the angel? How about his wife?

Lesson 83.
Samson
Judges 14 & 15

Background: *Samson is a difficult "hero of the faith" for me. His parents don't seem to be exactly the brightest set in scripture. Samson himself seems to be a body the Spirit uses every now and then to knock some Philistines around. Perhaps these passages show us just how far Israel had fallen at this point. God uses Samson to judge the Philistines, but I want to encourage my children to take a close, critical look at Samson's character. Since God teaches through negative as well as positive examples, I want to teach my children how to tell the difference.*

Chapter 14

1. Is Samson's attitude toward his parents respectful? Does he ask their advice?

2. What objection do his parents make to his marrying a Philistine woman?

Reminder: *What had the Philistines been doing for 40 years? What had God said about marrying the daughters of the land?*

3. What enables Samson to kill the lion with his bare hands?

4. What do we learn about Samson's character from these incidents?

5. Was it fair for the Philistines to attempt to find out the answer by appealing to Samson's wife?

6. *Picture the scene: The feast to celebrate their wedding is in full swing, and Samson's new wife has been weeping for the whole seven days of the feast...* How do you think Samson feels?

7. How does Samson pay off his bet with the Philistines?

8. What happened to Samson's Philistine wife?

Chapter 15

9. How does Samson react when his wife's father refused to let him visit her?

10. How do the Philistines react to Samson's vengeance? How does Judah react to the demands of the Philistines that they surrender Samson?

11. What enables Samson to kill a thousand men with the jawbone of an ass?

Lesson 84.
Samson and Delilah
Judges 16

Background: *The major failures in Samson's life involve strange women. First, the Philistine woman of Timnah whom he wanted to marry, then the harlot of Gaza, then Delilah of Sorek.*

1. Discuss Samson's choice of women. This might be a useful time to do a study in Proverbs on the topic of "strange women."

2. How does Samson escape from the city of Gaza?

Background: *At dusk, each city locked their gates and often posted guards. No one was allowed in or out until the gates reopened at daylight. The gates were built to be strong enough to withstand a besieging army.*

3. Three times, Delilah entices Samson and begs for the secret of his strength. Three times he tricks her. Three times the men waiting to ambush him must remain in hiding. The question is, why didn't Samson get suspicious?

4. Why are the Philistines able to bind Samson? *Hint: There was nothing magic about Samson's hair. What was the hair a sign and symbol of?*

5. Why does Samson's strength return during the feast to Dagon?

6. What does Samson accomplish with his death?

7. How does Samson compare with the other judges you have studied?

Lesson 85.
Naomi loses Husband and Sons
Ruth 1 & 2

Chapter 1

1. What nationality are Naomi and her husband Elimelech? Why do they move to Moab?

2. What nationality are Orpah and Ruth?

3. What happened to Elimelech and his sons?

4. How do Orpah and Ruth react when Naomi tells them to return to Moab?

Chapter 2

5. What is Boaz's reaction when Ruth comes to glean his field? What does Boaz know about Ruth?

6. What do we learn about Boaz' character from the way he treats Ruth?

Background: *Look up Matthew 1:5 to see who Boaz's mother was.*

Lesson 86.
Boaz Redeems Ruth
Ruth 3 & 4

Chapter 3

1. What instructions does Naomi give Ruth? How does Ruth respond?

2. What specific traits does Boaz praise Ruth for? What does he say about her reputation?

3. What does Boaz promise to do?

4. What do Naomi and Ruth do while waiting for Boaz to fulfill his promise?

Chapter 4

5. Why does the "closest relative" decline to redeem the land of Elimelech and marry Ruth? Does this same possibility concern Boaz?

6. Who do the elders compare Ruth? What example do they hope she will imitate?

7. Who is descended from Ruth and Boaz?

Lesson 87.
Hannah and Eli
1 Samuel 1 & 2

Chapter 1

1. Describe Hannah's relationship with her husband. Why does Hannah's husband give her a double portion at the festivals?

2. Why does Hannah have no children?

3. When Eli saw Hannah at Shiloh, what does he think was wrong with her?

4. What does Samuel's name mean?

5. What does Hannah do to show her gratitude to God for answering her prayer?

6. According to Hannah's prayer, what does God honor?

Chapter 2

7. What kind of men are Eli's sons?

8. Who enables Hannah to have more children after Samuel?

9. How does Eli react to the reports of his sons wickedness?

10. Contrast Samuel with Eli's sons.

11. How does Eli honor his sons above the LORD?

12. What prophecy does the man of God make to Eli? (The prophecy is about both Eli and the Messiah who is to come).

Lesson 88.
Samuel's First Vision
1 Samuel 3 & 4

1. How does the passage describe God's communication with men in Israel at this time?

2. What does Samuel hear? How does Samuel discover who is actually calling him?

3. What does God tell Samuel he is about to do?

4. When Israel is defeated in the first battle with the Philistines, what plan do the elders of Israel make?

5. Does the presence of the ark insure Israel's victory over the Philistines? Why/why not?

6. What happens to the ark? How do the Philistines feel about the God of Israel?

7. What happens to the sons of Eli?

8. What happens to Eli when he heard the news?

9. Why is the ark of God taken?

Lesson 89.
The Philistines and the Ark
1 Samuel 5 & 6

1. How does Dagon "react" to the presence of the ark of the LORD? Why? What point is God making?

2. What happens to the Ashdodites because of the presence of the ark?

3. What happens when the ark was brought to Gath?

Background: *Do you know who comes from Gath later on? Hint: He's ugly, tall, and mean.*

4. What happens when the ark was brought to Ekron?

5. What do the Philistines do to remove the wrath of God from them?

Lesson 90.
Samuel judges Israel
1 Samuel 7 & 8

Chapter 7

1. What does Samuel command Israel to do in order to return to the LORD?

2. What is the result of Samuel's first military encounter with the Philistines?

Chapter 8

3. Describe Samuel's sons. How do they compare with Eli's sons?

4. What do the people want because of the wickedness of Samuel's sons?

5. What does Samuel warn Israel that a king will do? Review Deuteronomy 17:14-20.

6. Why do the people say they want a king? How does Samuel respond? How does God respond?

Lesson 91
Samuel anoints Saul
1 Samuel 9 & 10

1. What distinguishes Saul from the other Benjamites?

2. Why do Saul and his servant decide to visit Samuel?

3. What has God revealed to Samuel before Saul's visit?

4. After Samuel anoints Saul, what sign does he tell Saul to look for on his way home?

5. What happens when Saul meets the band of prophets?

6. When Samuel gathers Israel at Mizpah to present Saul to them, what happens? Why can't Saul be found? What does this tell us about Saul?

7. Does all Israel acknowledge Saul as king? What are their reasons? Who follows and who doesn't?

Lesson 92.
Saul leads Israel
to deliver Jabesh-gilead
Samuel charges Israel
1 Samuel 11 & 12

Chapter 11

1. What happens to Saul when he hears the appeal of the men of Jabesh-gilead? (this should ring echoes from the story of Samson)

2. How does Israel respond to Saul's appeal?

3. To whom does Saul give the credit for victory?

Chapter 12

4. Does anyone in Israel have a complaint against Samuel?

5. What choice does God set before Israel and the king?

Lesson 93.
Saul's Disobedience
1 Samuel 13 & 14

Background: *After initial victories by Saul and his son Jonathan, the Philistines are enraged and assemble to defeat Israel. Saul and his army are waiting for Samuel... seven days have passed and Samuel has not appeared...*

Chapter 13

1. What does Saul do when Samuel does not arrive?

2. What does Samuel say when he discovers what Saul has done?

Chapter 14

Background: *This can be a somewhat confusing and obscure chapter. There are at least three different stories woven together. One is the story of Jonathan's successful raid which spread rapidly and turned into a rout of the Philistines. The second is the story of Saul's oath imposed on Israel not to eat, unwittingly violated by Jonathan, Jonathan's discovery and his defense by the people of Israel. The third story is of the people of Israel forgetting God's decrees and falling on the spoil of the Philistine, slaughtering and eating calves and oxen and eating them without first draining the blood away - one of the fundamental articles of purity in the mosaic law.*

3. Why do Jonathan and his armor-bearer stage a 2-man raid on the Philistines? What does Jonathan say about their chances?

4. What happened that called attention to Jonathan's absence?

5. What vow does Saul make? What other vow does this remind you of?

6. What sin do the people commit after the victory over the Philistines? How does Saul atone for their sin?

7. How is Jonathan's violation of Saul's vow discovered?

8. What prevents Saul from carrying out this vow?

9. Compare Saul with Jephthah.

Lesson 94.
Saul sins and lies, Samuel confronts
1 Samuel 15

1. When Saul defeated the Amalekites, what was he supposed to have done? What did he do?

2. What does God say to Samuel about Saul?

3. What does Samuel tell Saul he has done? Is he truthful?

4. What does Samuel say when Saul acknowledges his sin?

Lesson 95.
David anointed as Saul's Successor
1 Samuel 16

1. Why does God send Samuel to Bethlehem?

2. What does God say when Samuel suspects that the chosen one is Jesse's eldest son, Eliab?

3. What has happened to David since he was anointed by Samuel?

4. What change occurs with Saul at the same time?

5. What do Saul's servants recommend?

6. What position does David assume at Saul's court?

Lesson 96.
David and Goliath
1 Samuel 17

1. Who is Goliath? How big is he? What is his challenge to the army of Israel?

Background: *A cubit is approximately 18 inches. Calculate Goliath's height with your children. Give them some real object of comparable height to look at while you read about Goliath.*

2. What is the reaction of "Saul and all Israel?" see also verse 24

Background: *Remember, Saul was distinguished at his anointing because he stood a head taller than any other in Israel... Moral: There's always someone taller...*

3. How does David's oldest brother, Eliab react to his visit and his questions about Goliath?

4. What military experience does David cite to Saul?

5. Who does he give the credit for his victories over lion and bear?

6. Why does David reject Saul's armor?

7. What is Goliath's reaction when he sees David?

8. What prophecy does David make to Goliath? Who does he say will win and why?

9. What does the Philistine army do when they see David kill Goliath? Do they keep their bargain?

Lesson 97.
David and Jonathan
1 Samuel 18 & 19

1. What reaction might have been expected from the son of the king when someone else's son won a great victory?

2. How does Jonathan feel about David?

3. What does Jonathan do to demonstrate his affection for David?

4. How does Saul react to the people's celebration of David's victory?

5. Does Saul really want David to be his son-in-law?

6. What does Saul want from David as a dowry for his daughter Michal?

7. What does Saul hope will happen to David?

8. How does Saul feel about David?

9. How does David behave as a commander in Saul's army?

10. Why does Jonathan disobey his father and warn David?

11. Why does Michal disobey her father and warn David?

Background: *At this point, if you have time, you might enjoy reading Psalm 59, whose heading declares "when Saul sent men, and they watched the house in order to kill him."*

The incident with three sets of messengers and finally Saul himself overtaken by the spirit of God and prophesying is very puzzling. It served to prevent Saul from capturing and executing David and that may be its only meaning.

Lesson 98.
David and Jonathan
1 Samuel 20

1. How much does David trust Jonathan?

2. What promise does Jonathan ask of David?

3. What is Saul's reaction when Jonathan announces that David has left to sacrifice with his family in Bethlehem?

4. What does David say it would mean if this news angered Saul?

5. What does Saul accuse Jonathan of having done? Are his suspicions accurate?

6. Does Jonathan keep his promise to David?

<h1>Lesson 99.</h1>

David flees into Exile
1 Samuel 21 & 22

Chapter 21

1. What help does David ask of the priest at Nob? Does he tell him the truth about where he is going and why he is alone?

2. Was it right for David to eat of the consecrated shewbread?
    This is a bit of a trick question, since we have Jesus' own pronouncement on the matter in Mark 2:23-28. Jesus cites David's eating of the shewbread as precedent and example for his own eating of grain from the fields on a sabbath.

3. What else does David receive from the priest at Nob?
    Remember the name, Doeg the Edomite, chief of Saul's shepherds. He will appear again...

4. Why does David pretend to be mad in the presence of the king of Achish?

Background: *At this point, if you have time, you might enjoy reading **Psalm 34** "Of David. When he pretended to be insane before Abimelech, who drove him away and he left."*

Chapter 22

4. Why does David send his parents to Moab (descendants of Lot)?
    Hint: Who was his great-grandmother? See Matthew 1:5-6.

5. What charge does Saul level at his servants and the rest of his tribe (Benjamin)?

6. What charge does he make against the priest Ahimelech?

7. What does Saul command his servants to do to the priests? Do they obey?

8. What does Doeg the Edomite do?

Background: *See also Psalm 52 "When Doeg the Edomite had gone to Saul and told him: 'David has gone to the house of Ahimelech.'"*

Lesson 100.
Saul hunts David in the Wilderness
1 Samuel 23 & 24

Chapter 23

1. Why does David go to Keilah? Why does Saul go to Keilah?

2. Are the people of Keilah grateful to David for delivering them from the Philistines?

3. How do David and Jonathan renew their covenant?

4. Who seeks to betray David to Saul?

Background: *See also* **Psalm 54** *"A maskil of David. When the Ziphites had gone to Saul and said, 'Is not David hiding among us?'"*

5. David narrowly escapes being captured by Saul. What happened?

Background: *This might be a fun scene to act out. Select an appropriate piece of furniture to represent the mountain and have Saul and his men approaching on one side, while David and his men are hidden on the other. You get the idea.*

Chapter 24

6. Another close escape. But is it David or Saul who escapes?

7. Why doesn't David strike Saul? Why does he feel guilty about cutting the edge of Saul's robe?

8. Why does David confront Saul outside the cave?

9. How does Saul react to David's plea? What prophecy does Saul repeat concerning David?

10. What does David promise Saul?

Lesson 101.
David and Abigail
1 Samuel 25

1. Why does David send his men to Nabal at shearing time?

2. How have David and his men behaved towards Nabal and his shepherds?

3. How does Nabal react to David's request?

4. What is Abigail's reaction when she learns how Nabal has acted?

5. What does Abigail ask David for?

6. What is David's response to Abigail?

7. What is Nabal doing while Abigail is pleading for his life with David?

8. What happens when Abigail explains to Nabal what has happened?

9. What does David do when he hears of Nabal's death?

Lesson 102.
David spares Saul again
1 Samuel 26

1. Why is Saul seeking to kill David again?

2. Why does David not kill Saul in his camp?

3. What charge does David make against Abner (Saul's cousin and army commander)?

4. What promise does Saul make to David this time?

5. Would you have trusted Saul?

Lesson 103.
David flees to the Philistines Saul consults a witch
1 Samuel 27-28

Chapter 27

1. Why does David leave Israel for Philistia?

2. Why does Achish believe David is now hated in Israel?

Chapter 28

3. What was Saul's reaction when the Philistines gathered together against Israel?

4. Why did Saul seek for a medium? How does God feel about seeking mediums? See Deuteronomy 18:9-12.

5. Why did he disguise himself for the visit?

6. What does Samuel say to Saul?

7. What is his prophecy about the coming battle?

8. What effect do Samuel's words have on Saul?

Lesson 104.
David turned back,
defeats the Amalekites
1 Samuel 29-30

Chapter 29

1. Why do the commanders of the Philistines object to David's presence with the army?

2. What is Achish (king of the Philistines) opinion of David's character?

Chapter 30

3. What has happened back in Ziklag during David's absence with the Philistine army?

4. What is David's reaction to the news? (and the men with him?)

5. What does David do before he sets out?

6. What do David and his men do for the Egyptian found (apparently lying ill in the fields)?

7. What happens when David catches up with the Amalekites?

8. What is the dispute between those who fought and those who stayed with the baggage?

9. What does David say should be done with the spoil? How should it be divided?

10. Who else does David send some of the spoil to? Why?

Lesson 105.

Death of Saul and Jonathan
1 Samuel 31 & 1 Chronicles 10

Background: *1 Samuel 31 is a straightforward report of Saul's defeat and death, and the death of his three sons with him. 1 Chronicles 10 repeats the same details, but then includes a summary of why Saul died:*

So Saul died for his trespass which he committed against the LORD, because of the word of the LORD which he did not keep; and also because he asked counsel of a medium, making inquiry of it, and did not inquire of the LORD. Therefore He killed him, and turned the kingdom to David the son of Jesse.

1. The key question that summarizes all of Saul's life then, is Why? Why did he disobey God? And what were the consequences of his disobedience?

Lesson 106.

David hears of the death of Saul and Jonathan
2 Samuel 1

Background: *With the death of Saul, the road is now open for David to become king. Evidently, someone thought the news of the death of Saul would be pleasing to him, perhaps that the person who had killed Saul might even be rewarded.*

Reminder: *Twice, David had the opportunity to kill Saul himself and had refused to do so, citing the principle: "Who can stretch out his hand against the Lord's anointed and be without guilt?" Also remember that the Amalekites had just kidnapped David's wives and carried them off into slavery, forcing him to pursue and fight to rescue them. Now, here comes an Amalekite announcing "I killed Saul!"*

1. Why might the Amalekite's testimony be unreliable? What did he hope to gain by claiming to have killed David's enemy?

2. How does David react to the news of Saul's (and Jonathan's) death?

3. What does he do to the Amalekite who claimed to have killed Saul?

Lesson 107.
David becomes King
2 Samuel 2

1. To which tribe does David return?

2. What does he say to the men who had buried Saul?

3. What happens to Ish-bosheth, Saul's fourth son?

4. Which men are leading the two armies in the civil war? What does each side hope to gain?

Lesson 108.
Civil War between David and the house of Saul
2 Samuel 3

1. Abner plots to betray Ish-bosheth, whom he has made king. Why?

2. What one thing does David want from Abner?

3. Why does Joab not trust Abner?

4. Why does Joab kill Abner?

5. How does David honor Abner after his death?

Lesson 109.
Death of Ish-bosheth, Saul's Son
2 Samuel 4

1. How does Ish-bosheth react to news of the death of Abner?

2. Who kills Ish-bosheth?

3. What do they do after they kill him?

4. How does David react when Rechab and Baanah bring him news that they have killed Ish-bosheth?

Lesson 110.
David makes Jerusalem his Capital
2 Samuel 5-6

Chapter 5

1. David becomes greater and greater. Why?

2. What does David do before he goes into battle against the Philistines?

Chapter 6

3. Why is God displeased with Uzzah?

4. What is David's reaction to God's displeasure?

5. What happens to the household where the Ark rested?

6. What is Michal's reaction to David's dance before the Ark?

7. What happens to Michal as a result of her despising David?

Background: *You might also want to look at 1 Chronicles 13-15 for another account of these events.*

<h1>Lesson 111.</h1>

David wishes to build a Temple
The borders of David's conquests
2 Samuel 7-8

Chapter 7

1. What does David tell Nathan the prophet he wishes to do?

2. What message does God give Nathan for David? What does God say about building the temple? What does God say he will do for the "house of David?"

3. Who does God say will build the temple? Why?

4. What does God promise/prophesy concerning David's royal house?

5. How does David respond to God's message?

Chapter 8

6. How does David deal with the nations surrounding Israel? Why is he successful?

7. Find each of the nations whom David defeated on a map:
Philistines
Moab
Arameans of Damascus
Edom

"So David reigned over all Israel; and David administered justice and righteousness for all his people." **2 Samuel 8:15**

Lesson 112.
David and Mephibosheth
2 Samuel 9-10

Chapter 9

1. Why does David wish to show kindness to Saul's descendants? Why is this unusual?

2. What does David give to Mephibosheth?

3. What does he command Saul's servant Ziba to do for Mephibosheth?

4. What position of honor at David's table does he give to Mephibosheth?

Chapter 10

5. Why is David disposed kindly to the Ammonites and the son of king Hanun? (*cf. 1 Samuel 22:3 where Moab shelters David's parents - perhaps Ammon had offered some similar act of kindness during David's exile*)

6. How are David's messengers received? How does David respond?

Background: *Moab and Ammon are the descendants of Lot and his two daughters. Edom is the descendant of Esau.*

7. What does Joab say in his speech to the army of Israel?

8. Who wins the battle between Israel and the alliance of Arameans and Ammonites?

Lesson 113.
David and Bathsheba
2 Samuel 11-12

1. What, according to 2 Samuel, do kings usually do in the spring? What does David do?

2. When did David first begin to sin?
   When he saw Bathsheba? When he inquired as to who she was?
   When he sent messengers to her? When she came to him?
   When he lay with her?

3. Why does David ask his commander to send Uriah home from the battle?

4. Why does Uriah refuse to sleep in his house? How does this contrast with David's sense of responsibility?

5. Why does David command Joab to place Uriah in the fiercest part of the battle?

6. What does Bathsheba do after her husband's death?

7. When does Nathan come to David? How long has it been since David's initial sin?

8. Why does Nathan tell David the story of the two men? How does David react?

9. How does Nathan describe David's sin? What does he say the specific consequences of David's sin will be?

10. What is David's reaction to being confronted with his sin?

11. Why does Nathan say that David's child will die? What had David's deed caused?

12. When David's child is ill, what does he do?

13. After the child dies, how does David's behavior change? How does he explain the change?

14. What was the name of the second son of David and Bathsheba?

Background: *You might also want to read Psalm 51: "When the prophet Nathan came to him after David had committed adultery with Bathsheba."*

15. Why does Joab send for David to lead the armies to victory? Why does he not capture the city himself?

Lesson 114.
Amnon, Tamar, and Absalom
2 Samuel 13

"Behold, I will raise up evil against you from your own household"
2 Samuel 12:11

Background: *Note that Absalom and Tamar are full sister and brother, Amnon is the son of David and a different mother, he is a half-brother to Absalom and Tamar.*

The subject of this chapter may be a bit sensitive for your younger students. You have several options in dealing with this. You may simply want to read the chapter to your students and answer any questions that normally arise. This might be an opportunity to start a conversation on sensitive subjects in the context of what God teaches us in the Bible. You may also find that your students are satisfied with the simple understanding that Amnon did something bad to Tamar, and the details are unimportant to them. Be alert to the maturity of your students and remember — God gave us these stories for sound reasons.

1. How do Amnon's feelings toward his sister change after he violated her?

2. How does Absalom react to Tamar's report of what their half-brother had done?

3. What do David and Absalom do to Amnon to punish him for his actions?

4. How does Absalom take his revenge on Amnon?

Background: *Amnon was apparently the eldest son, and Absalom perhaps the second or third. His murder of his elder brother also placed him closer to the throne, perhaps even next in the line of succession.*

5. What does Absalom do after the murder of Amnon?

6. How does David react to the death of Amnon? to the flight of Absalom?

<h1 style="text-align:center">Lesson 115.</h1>

Joab intercedes for Absalom
2 Samuel 14

Background: *Like Nathan the prophet, the woman presents a case for judgement to David. His answer reveals that his emotions have clouded his judgement in his own case. As the case unfolds, David rapidly discerns who had sent the woman — Joab, his army commander.*

1. What story does Joab tell the woman to present to David?

2. When Absalom returns from exile to Jerusalem, are he and David reunited? Why not?

3. When Joab ignores Absalom's two summons, how does Absalom get his attention?

4. How long is Absalom back in Jerusalem before he is reunited with David?

<h1 style="text-align:center">Lesson 116.</h1>

Absalom's Rebellion
2 Samuel 15

Background: *Hebron is the capital city of the tribe of Judah.*

1. How does David react to the news of Absalom's rebellion in Hebron?

2. What do the Levites do with the Ark when David is leaving?

3. What does David say to do with the Ark?

4. Whom does David leave behind in Jerusalem?

Lesson 117.
David on the road away from Jerusalem
2 Samuel 16

1. Who is Ziba? Who is Mephibosheth?

2. What does Ziba bring to David on the road away from Jerusalem?

3. What does David do for Ziba in response?

4. Another servant of Saul, Shimei approaches David. How is his attitude different from Ziba's?

5. How does David react to the cursing of Shimei? What does he say to Abishai?

6. What is Absalom's reaction to seeing his father's counselor, Hushai?

7. To whom does Absalom turn for advice?

8. What advice does Ahithophel give?

Background: *You might also want to read Psalm 3, "A psalm of David. When he fled from his son Absalom."*

Lesson 118.
David and Absalom gather their Armies
2 Samuel 17

1. What request does Ahithophel make of Absalom?

2. What alternative does Hushai propose?

3. Why does Absalom follow the counsel of Hushai rather than Ahithophel?

4. How does David learn of the plans of Absalom?

5. Where do the two spies hide on their way from Jerusalem to David?

6. How does Ahithophel react when his counsel was ignored?

Lesson 119.
The Death of Absalom
2 Samuel 18

1. David appoints commanders over his army. When he proposes to lead the army into battle himself, how do the people react?

2. What special charge does David give to Joab concerning Absalom?

3. How does Joab react to the news that one of his servants has passed up an opportunity to kill Absalom?

Background: *Whoever brought news of a victory to the king was usually honored. Ahimaaz is the son of Zadok the high priest and one of the two spies who brought word of Absalom's plans from Jerusalem.*

4. Why does Joab NOT want Ahimaaz to carry the news of the victory to David?

5. How does David react to the news of Absalom's death?

Lesson 120.
Joab Rebukes David
2 Samuel 19

1. How do the people react to David's mourning over Absalom?

2. Why does Joab rebuke David?

3. What does Joab tell David he must do?

4. What office does David promise to Amasa of Judah? Who holds the office at the time? What role had Amasa played in Absalom's rebellion? (cf. 2 Samuel 17:25)

5. How does David deal with Shimei, now that he has won?

6. How does he deal with Mephibosheth?

7. Why do the men of Israel and the men of Judah quarrel?

Lesson 121.
Sheba's Rebellion
2 Samuel 20

Background: *Benjamin is the tribe of Saul...*

1. Which of the tribes of Israel follow Sheba? Which remain loyal to David?

2. Does Amasa respond promptly to David's call to summon the men of Judah?

3. Whom does David send to pursue Sheba? Whose men go to pursue Sheba?

4. What happens when Amasa came out to meet Joab and his men?

5. What objection does the woman of Abel Beth-maacah make to the presence of Joab and the army besieging the city?

6. What solution does Joab propose?

7. Did Joab honor his word to the woman?

Background: *2 Samuel 21-24 recounts several incidents from David's reign and record a Psalm by him. Chapter 22-23:7 is almost identical with Psalm 18. Chapter 21 records an incident in which God sends a famine to punish Israel for Saul's breaking of his oath to the Gibeonites. Chapter 23 records the names of the mighty men who fought with David. Chapter 24 records the census which David took in defiance of God's command, and God's subsequent judgement on Israel. Each of the elements in these chapters is worthy of study, but because they do not fit into the chronological recounting of the history of Israel, they are omitted from the study here.*

Lesson 122.

David, Solomon, and the Temple
1 Chronicles 22

1. Why does David begin the preparations for the temple that his son will build?

2. Why does David say (to Solomon) that God would not let him build the temple?

3. What qualities does David pray that God will give to Solomon?

4. What does David tell Solomon he must do if he is to prosper?

Lesson 123.

Solomon made heir to the Kingdom
1 Chronicles 28-29

Chapter 28

1. Once again, why does God not permit David to build the temple?

2. Why does David say that Solomon, among all his sons, is to be king after him?

Chapter 29

3. What is the response of the people of Israel to David's plans for the temple?

Lesson 124.
Adonijah rebels, David makes Solomon king
1 Kings 1

1. Who takes care of David in his old age?

2. What clue about Adonijah's character is given?

3. Who supports Adonijah's rebellion? Who opposes it?

4. What do Nathan and Bathsheba do to thwart Adonijah's rebellion?

5. How do Adonijah's supporters react to the proclamation of Solomon as king?

6. What does Adonijah do?

7. How does Solomon deal with Adonijah?

Lesson 125.
David dies,
Solomon deals with his Enemies
1 Kings 2

1. What is David's last charge to his son, Solomon?

2. What special instructions does David give concerning Joab? Why is Joab's murder of Abner and Amasa specially condemned?

3. What request does Adonijah make of Bathsheba after David's death?

Background: *This request, aside from being presumptuous, constitutes a claim to the throne, because of the close connection between Abishag and David.*

4. Why does Solomon say he will spare the life of Abiathar?

5. Why does Joab flee?

6. Why does Solomon say that Joab is guilty of?

7. What is Solomon's judgement on Shimei (the Benjamite who cursed David)?

8. Does Shimei keep his oath?

9. What happens when Shimei breaks his oath?

<h1 style="text-align:center">Lesson 126.</h1>

Solomon asks for Wisdom
1 Kings 3

1. Who does Solomon ally himself with by marriage?
   (Oh how far we've come from Moses & Joshua!)

2. When God appears to Solomon, how does he describe himself?

3. What does Solomon ask God to give him?

4. What does God promise to give to Solomon?

5. What does the story of the two women illustrate about Solomon?

Chapter four is a list of the officials appointed by Solomon to various offices. It is omitted from the list of readings.

<h2 style="text-align:center">Lesson 127.</h2>

The Building of the Temple
1 Kings 5-7

1. To whom does Solomon attribute the fact that Israel is at peace?

2. What does Solomon ask of Hiram, king of Tyre?

3. How does Hiram respond?

Background: *Chapter 6 & 7 describe the dimensions and furnishings of the temple built by Solomon.*

*This would be the perfect opportunity to do some research on the appearance of Solomon's temple. There are articles in many Bibles (often an illustration), in Bible dictionaries, in some encyclopedias and in such books as **The Cultural Atlas of the Bible**.*

Maps: *Map #9 of **The Student Bible Atlas** shows the kingdom of Solomon.*

The Dedication of the Temple
1 Kings 8-9:9

1. What happens when the Ark of the Covenant is moved by the priests into the Holy of Holies in the new temple?

Background: *Try outlining the major sections of Solomon's prayer. It ties together everything having to do with the welfare of Israel and the people and acknowledges God's sovereignty and the centrality of prayer, either in the temple or towards the temple (i.e. towards God).*

    I. If a man sins and takes an oath before Thine altar...

    II. When thy people Israel are defeated before an enemy make supplication to thee in this house

    III. When the heavens are shut up and there is no rain

    IV. If there is famine in the land spreading his hands toward this house the foreigner... when he comes and prays toward this house.

    V. When thy people go out to battle against their enemy...

    VI. When they sin against Thee

You might also want to look at the parallel account in 2 Chronicles 7:1-3.

Chapter 9:1-9

2. What is God's response to Solomon's prayer?

3. What is God's promise of blessing for obedience?

4. What is God's promise of judgement for disobedience?

The rest of the chapter is a list of public works and city building which Solomon undertakes.

Lesson 129.
Solomon's Kingdom
1 Kings 10

1. How does the Queen of Sheba test Solomon?

2. What about Solomon impresses her?

3. How far does Solomon's reputation for wisdom and wealth extend?

Lesson 130.
The End of Solomon's Reign
1 Kings 11

1. What problem do all of Solomon's foreign wives cause?

2. What specific things does Solomon do which displease God?

3. What does God say will happen to Solomon and his house because of his idolatry?

4. Who raised up adversaries against Solomon?

5. What prophecy does Ahijah make to Jeroboam?

6. Why does God say this is going to happen?

Lesson 131.
Rehoboam and Jeroboam
1 Kings 12

Background: *At this point, we suggest you begin a chart of the kings of Israel and Judah. At the top of your chart you can start with the three kings of the united kingdom, Saul, David and Solomon. Underneath Solomon you can begin two columns, one for Judah and one for Israel. We use a color-coding scheme to keep track of God's view of things. Kings whom God praises we write in blue, kings whom God calls wicked we write in black. It won't take long before the dominance of black in the line of the kings of Israel will cause your students to make some comments. We also add occasional illustrations to show significant facts about certain kings. A bright red flame for those kings who worshiped Molech by sacrificing their own sons, and lightning bolts to represent the ministries of important prophets.*

You may find the chart of the kings on the next page helpful, but we encourage you to make your own chart as well.

1. What request/demand does Jeroboam place before Rehoboam on behalf of Israel?

2. What counsel do the elders give Rehoboam? Does he take it?

3. Who does Rehoboam listen to?

4. What does Israel do when Rehoboam gives them his harsh reply?

5. What does Israel do when Rehoboam sent Adoram to them?

6. What happens when Rehoboam prepared for civil war with Jeroboam?

7. Why is Jeroboam concerned about Israel going to Jerusalem? What does he do?

8. Who does he appoint as priests to the golden calves?

9. What happened the last time Israel worshiped golden calves?

Lesson 132.
Jeroboam's Idolatry
1 Kings 13

1. What prophecy does the man of God make concerning the altars at Bethel?

2. What happens when Jeroboam tries to seize the man of God?

3. How does the man of God respond to Jeroboam's invitation?

4. What does the old prophet at Bethel tell the man of God?

5. What happens to the man of God?

6. What was Jeroboam's response to the prophecy, and his illness and healing?

Lesson 133.
Abijah dies, Rehoboam turns to Idolatry
1 Kings 14

1. Who does Jeroboam turn to when his son becomes ill?

2. What is Ahijah's prophecy concerning Jeroboam's house? concerning his son? Why will these calamities occur?

3. What does Judah do under Rehoboam?

4. What does the King of Egypt do to Jerusalem and the temple?

The Kings of Judah and Israel

Saul

David

Solomon

Judah

Israel

1060
1040
1020
1000
980
960
940
920
900
880
860
840
820
800
780
760
740
720
700
680
660
640
620
600
580
560
540
520
500

Rehoboam

Abijah(Abijam)

Asa

Jehoshaphat

Jehoram
Ahaziah
Queen Athaliah

Joash

Amaziah

Uzziah
(Azariah)

Jotham

Ahaz

Hezekiah

Manasseh

Amon

Josiah

Jehoahaz
Jehoiakim
Jehoiachin
Zedekiah

Jeroboam

Nadab

Baasha

Elah
Zimri

Omri

Ahab

Ahaziah

Jehoram

Jehu

Jehoahaz

Jehoash

Jeroboam II

Zechariah
Shallum

Pekah

Menahem
Pekahiah

Hoshea

Dispersed by Assyria

Captivity in Babylon

© copyright, 1994 Greenleaf Press

Lesson 134.
Abijam, King of Judah
1 Kings 15:1-7
2 Chronicles 13

1 Kings 15:1-7 Abijam of Judah (part 1)

1. Is Rehoboam's son better or worse than his father?

2. Why does God bless Rehoboam's son, Abijam?

2 Chronicles 13 Abijam of Judah (part 2)

3. What charges does Abijam make against Israel and Jeroboam?

4. Who has the larger army, Israel or Judah?

5. Who has the element of surprise in the battle?

6. Who wins the battle? Why?

Lesson 135.
Asa, King of Judah
2 Chronicles 14-16

Chapter 14

1. What is God's judgement on King Asa?

2. What does Asa do that pleases God?

3. Who does Asa turn to for help when threatened by King Baasha of Israel?

4. Who has the larger army, Ethiopia or Judah?

5. What does Asa ask God to do?

6. Who wins? Who defeats the Ethiopians?

Chapter 15

7. What message does Azariah bring to Israel and Asa?

8. How does Asa respond to Azariah's message?

9. How do Judah and Benjamin respond to Azariah's message?

Chapter 16

10. Who does Asa turn to when Judah is threatened by King Baasha of Israel?

11. What does Hanani the seer say to Asa about his alliance?

12. How does Asa's action differ from the way he met the army of Ethiopia?

13. Who does Asa turn to when he becomes ill?

Nadab, Baasha, Elah, Zimri, Omri, Ahab — Kings of Israel
1 Kings 15:25-16

Background: *These verses record the reigns of 6 kings of Israel (7 if you count Omri's rival, Tibni). Make sure you add each one to your chart, indicate whether his reign pleased God or not and also, the length of his reign.*

1. What is God's opinion of Nadab's rule?

2. How does Baasha become king?

3. What does Baasha do to the relatives of Jeroboam?

4. What is God's opinion of Baasha's rule?

5. How long does Elah, Baasha's son rule?

6. What is God's opinion of Elah's rule?
   (you may have to skip down to verse 13)

7. How does Zimri become king?

8. What does Zimri do to the relatives of Baasha?

9. How long does Zimri rule?

10. How does Omri become king? What office did he hold before becoming king?

11. What is God's opinion of Omri's rule?

12. How does Ahab become king?

13. Is Ahab better or worse than his father? What does Ahab do that was worse? What is wrong with marrying Jezebel?

14. What is God's opinion of Ahab's rule?

Lesson 137.
Elijah of Israel
Famine and the Widow's Child
1 Kings 17

1. What message does Elijah bring to Ahab? Why is God causing a drought in Israel?

2. How does God manage to provide food and water for Elijah?

3. What does Elijah have to do?

4. What complaint does the woman make when Elijah asked her for food?

5. Does she do what Elijah tells her?

6. What does the woman accuse Elijah of when her son dies?

7. What effect does the healing of her son have on the widow?

Maps: *Map #12 of **The Student Bible Atlas** shows the locations of major events in Elijah's life.*

Lesson 138.
Elijah and the prophets of Baal
1 Kings 18

1. Who is Obadiah? What office does he hold? What is his character? What has he done to demonstrate where his allegiance lies?

2. Why does Obadiah fear to carry out Elijah's request?

3. How does Ahab greet Elijah?

4. What does Elijah command Ahab to do?

5. What question does Ahab pose to Israel? How do the people answer?

6. How does Elijah address the prophets of Baal when their efforts prove unsuccessful?

7. Why does Elijah soak his offering with water?

Background: *In Hebrew, the phrase "The LORD, He is God" is "eli-jah!"*

8. What does Elijah do to the prophets of Baal? Why?

Lesson 139.
Elijah, Jezebel, and Elisha
1 Kings 19

1. How does Jezebel respond to the news of Elijah's actions on Mount Carmel?

2. Find Beersheba on the map. How far is it from Mt. Carmel and Jezreel?

3. How does God provide food and water for Elijah?

4. What is Elijah's complaint to God?

5. How does God respond?

6. Who does God tell Elijah to anoint?

7. How does Elisha respond to Elijah's casting of his mantle on him?

Lesson 140.
Ahab and Ben-Hadad
1 Kings 20

1. What does Ben-hadad threaten to do to Israel and the city of Samaria?

2. What message does the man of God have for Ahab?

3. Why does God say he will give the victory to Ahab?

4. Why do the servants of King Ben-hadad think they lost the battle to Israel?

5. What message does the man of God have for Ahab about the second invasion?

6. How does Ahab deal with the defeated King Ben-hadad?

7. Like Nathan before David, the man of God tells Ahab a story...
   What should be done to a soldier who fails to carry out his orders?

8. How does Ahab react to the rebuke delivered by the man of God?
   What does this show about him?

Lesson 141.
Jezebel Murders Naboth, Ahab Repents
1 Kings 21

1. Is there anything wrong with Ahab's original proposal to Naboth to buy or trade for his vineyard?

2. How does Ahab react to Naboth's refusal to sell?

3. In whose name, on whose authority, does Jezebel plot against Naboth?

4. Why does Jezebel have to enlist two worthless men to lie about Naboth?

5. Which two commandments has Ahab broken in his dealings with Naboth?

6. What does Elijah say will happen to Ahab? to Ahab's house? to Jezebel?

7. What is Ahab's reaction to Elijah's pronouncement?

8. How does God modify his judgement based on Ahab's humbling of himself?

Lesson 142.
False prophets and the death of Ahab God's view of Jehoshophat & Ahaziah
1 Kings 22

1. What does Ahab propose to Jehoshophat that they should do?

2. What does Jehoshophat ask Ahab to do before they proceed?

3. What do the 400 prophets proclaim as the Lord's word to Ahab?

4. What does Micaiah say?

5. Why do you suppose Ahab disguises himself before the battle? Do you think he secretly fears that Micaiah was right?

6. How is Ahab killed?

7. What is God's judgement on Jehoshophat? Is he like his father Asa, or not?

8. What is God's judgement on Ahaziah? Is he like his father Ahab?

Lesson 143.
Jehoshophat of Judah
2 Chronicles 17-19

1. Why does God judge favorably on Jehoshophat's reign?

2. What specifically does he do (and not do) that pleased God?

3. What does Jehoshophat do to establish God's law in the cities of Judah?

Background: *Chapter 18 is a parallel account of the alliance with Ahab leading to war with Ben-hadad and the death of Ahab. Make sure your students recall the main points and then proceed to chapter 19.*

4. Why does Jehu rebuke Jehoshophat?

5. Jehoshophat has already taken two steps to strengthen the cities of Judah. In 17:2 he places troops, in 17:9 he sends a delegation to teach the book of the law. What third step does he now take for the cities of Judah?

6. What charge does Jehoshophat give to the judges?

Lesson 144.
Jehoshophat at war with Moab
2 Chronicles 20

1. How does Jehoshophat respond when threatened by the armies of Moab and Ammon? What did he do first?

2. Jehoshophat's prayer quotes part of Solomon's prayer at the dedication of the temple (cf. 2 Chronicles 6:28-30). What does Jehoshophat ask God to do?

3. What answer does God send to Jehoshophat's prayer?

   2 Chronicles 20:20 is the rallying cry of a righteous leader encouraging his people! We need leaders who would lead us in this fashion! [end of editorial comment.]

4. Who does Jehoshophat appoint to go out ahead of the army?

5. How do Jehoshophat and his army defeat their enemies?

6. Jehoshophat also allies himself with Ahab's son Ahaziah, the king of Israel. What was God's opinion of the alliance?

Lesson 145.
Ahaziah inquires of Baal-zebub, Elijah Answers
2 Kings 1

1. What does Ahaziah do to find out if he will recover from his injury?

2. Who meets Ahaziah's messengers on their way to inquire of Baal-zebub? What answer does he give to Ahaziah's question?

3. What happens to the messengers Ahaziah sent to bring Elijah back?

Background: *Now this may get a little confusing... Ahab's second son is named Jehoram and he succeeds his elder brother Ahaziah and becomes king of Israel. After a four year overlap with King Jehoshophat of Judah, Jehoshophat dies and leaves the kingdom of Judah to his son, ALSO named Jehoram. It's easy to confuse them. One is Jehoram of Israel, son of Ahab; the other is Jehoram of Judah, son of Jehoshophat.*

Unfortunately, it gets worse. Jehoram of Judah has a son, and names him Ahaziah, the same name born by the elder brother of Jehoram of Israel. To see the sequence of kings and overlap of names, see the chart, The Kings of Judah and Israel on page 105.

We'll take up their stories in later lessons. But first, we return to the story of Elijah and Elisha...

Lesson 146.

Elisha receives the mantle of Elijah
2 Kings 2

Background: *Elijah and Elisha visit two of the "schools of the prophets" at Bethel and at Jericho. At each place, the prophets inquire of Elisha, "Do you know that the LORD will take away your master from over you today?" But Elisha already knows...*

1. How do Elijah and Elisha get across the Jordan?

2. What is Elisha's request of Elijah before he departs?

3. How does Elisha get back across the Jordan?

4. Why do the prophets wish to send out a search party to look for Elijah?

5. How does Elisha change the spring water in the city of the prophets?

6. What happens to the youths of Bethel who come out to mock Elisha?

Lesson 147.

Jehoram & Jehoshophat defeat Moab
2 Kings 3

1. Is Jehoram of Israel a good king or a bad king?
    (Are you keeping track of the good and bad kings on your chart?)

2. Who does Jehoram of Israel ask for help when Moab rebels?

3. When the three kings come to Elisha, does he welcome all three of them?

4. Why would he have no regard for the king of Israel?

5. What does Elisha do to provide for the army of the three kings?

6. Why does God give a victory over Moab to the three kings? (Judah, Israel, and Edom)

Lesson 148.
Elisha and the Shunamite's Son
2 Kings 4

1. What connection does the woman have with Elisha?

2. What does she say about her dead husband?

3. How does the prophet's widow demonstrate her faith?

4. What does the Shunamite woman do for Elisha?

5. What does he offer to do for her by way of thanks?

6. What does Gehazi suggest?

7. What does Elisha prophesy will happen for her?

8. How does the Shunamite show her faith when her son died?

9. What does Elisha do for the Shunamite? What part does Gehazi play?

10. How is the Shunamite's son revived?

11. What does Elisha do to change the stew to make it safe?

Elisha's distribution of the first fruits of grain prefigures and parallels Jesus' feeding of the five thousand in the Gospels.

Lesson 149.
Naaman's Leprosy Healed, Gehazi Cursed
2 Kings 5

Background: *Aram is the land of the Arameans, with its capital at Damascus in what is now Syria. The name of the king of Israel in this story is not given, but it is either Jehu or Jehoahaz whom we will study in the next few lessons.*

1. What is Namaan's position?

2. What is the reaction of the king of Israel to the letter from the king of Aram? Why doesn't he seek out Elisha? Why does Elisha have to send word to him?

3. What does Elisha tell Naaman to do? How does Naaman react to Elisha's instructions? What do his servants counsel him? What happens?

4. What change does Naaman say he will make in his behavior when he goes home?

5. Why does Gehazi pursue Naaman as he is leaving?

6. What does he say to Naaman? Is this true?

7. What does he say to Elisha? Is this true?

8. What happened to Gehazi? What did he get from Naaman besides silver and cloth? *Another of God's little ironies...*

Lesson 150.
Famine and War in Samaria
2 Kings 6 & 7

1. What does Elisha do to retrieve the borrowed axe that fell into the Jordan?

2. Why is the king of Aram angry at Elisha? What has Elisha done?
"Do not fear, for those who are with us are more than those who are with them."
2 Kings 6:16

This story always makes me wonder about the things we would see if only we have our eyes opened!

3. What does Elisha do with the army of the king of Aram?

4. How bad is the siege and famine in Samaria?

5. What does the king of Israel attempt to do about the famine?

6. What prophecy does Elisha make about the duration of the famine?

7. What further prophecy does Elisha make to the royal officer who doubted Elisha's prophecy?

8. What does God do in the camp of the Arameans?

9. What is the FIRST reaction of the lepers who find the camp of the Arameans? What is their SECOND reaction?

10. What does the king think has happened to the Arameans?

11. What happens to the royal official who doubted Elisha?

Lesson 151.
Elisha's Prophecy to Hazael
Jehoram king of Judah
2 Kings 8

1. Why does Elisha warn the Shunamite woman? How does she (once again) demonstrate her faith?

2. How does she get her land back after she returns from the Philistines?

3. What reputation does Elisha have in Damascus with the king of the Arameans? What had Elisha done that the Arameans might have heard of? *(Remember Naaman!)*

4. What vision does Elisha receive concerning Hazael?

5. How does Hazael confirm Elisha's estimation of his character?

6. Jehoshophat's son, Jehoram of Judah now becomes king. Is he a good king? What is his connection with Israel and Ahab and Jezebel?

7. Ahaziah of Judah succeeds his father Jehoram as king. What is his mother's name? Who are his grandmother and grandfather on his mother's side?

8. Is he a good king?

9. Who does he ally himself with?

Background: *During the reign of Jehoram of Judah, the prophet Obadiah wrote the book that bears his name. One chapter long, it is particularly addressed to Edom which had rebelled against Judah at this time. It prophesies God's judgement on Edom and his vindication of Israel.*

Lesson 152.
Elisha Anoints Jehu
death of Jehoram and Jezebel
2 Kings 9

1.   Why does Elisha's assistant say that God has chosen Jehu to be the king of Israel?

2.   What has Ahab (and Jezebel) done?

3.   How does Jehu react to being anointed as the new king? Is he timid? Does he hesitate?

4.   Where does Jehu kill Joram, king of Israel? What is the significance of this place?

5.   Why does Jehu kill Ahaziah, king of Judah as well?

6.   Why does Jezebel call Jehu by the name Zimri?
     (cf. 1 Kings 15 if you need to review the story of Zimri)

7.   What happens to Jezebel?

Jehu Executes Judgement
2 Kings 10

"So Jehu killed all who remained of the house of Ahab in Jezreel, and all his great men and his acquaintances and his priests, until he left him without a survivor."
2 Kings 10:11

Review 1 Kings 21:19-26 to recall Elijah's pronouncement of God's judgement on Ahab.

1. How does Jehu manage to gather all the worshipers of Baal?

2. What does Jehu do to all those who kept the solemn feast to Baal?

3. What do they do with the temple that had been built to Baal?

4. Was God pleased with all Jehu had done? Why?

Lesson 154.

Athaliah and Joash
2 Kings 11

Background: *Remember, Athaliah is the daughter of Ahab and Jezebel.*

1. When Athaliah kills all of the royal offspring, who is she killing? How is she related to them?

2. Who hides Joash from Athaliah?

3. How long is he kept hidden?

4. Who rallies the captains to the cause of Joash?

5. What does Jehoiada do after the death of Athaliah?

6. Is Athaliah popular with the people of Jerusalem?

Lesson 155.
Joash Repairs the Temple
2 Kings 12
2 Chronicles 24:15-27

1. Would you call Joash a good king? Why or why not?

2. How are money offerings handled under Jehoiada?

3. Who has responsibility to keep the temple in good repair? Have they carried out their responsibilities?

4. What change in the handling of money does Joash establish?

5. Is there enough money to repair the temple?

6. What happens to all the treasures and wealth of the temple under the reign of Joash?

7. In what ways does Joash change after the death of Jehoiada?

8. What prophecy does Zechariah the son of Jehoiada make? How does Joash react?

9. How many men does Joash take into battle against the Arameans? How many men do the Arameans have? Who would you expect to win? Who wins?

10. How does Joash die?

Background: *It is during the reign of Joash that the prophet Joel writes the book of prophecy that bears his name. Its three chapters deal with God's recent judgement on Judah by a plague of locusts, his coming judgement for the nations ongoing sins, and a prophecy of God's blessings in a future restoration. It is worth reading here if you have time. If you study it later, remember to set it in the context of Athaliah's usurpation and Jehoiada's restoration of Joash.*

Lesson 156.
Jehoahaz & Jehoash of Israel, death of Elisha
2 Kings 13

Meanwhile, back in Israel (leaving Judah for a chapter)...

1. Is Jehoahaz a good king? Why or why not?

2. What does Jehoahaz do when Israel is oppressed by Hazael and Ben-hadad, kings of the Arameans?

3. How does God respond to Jehoahaz' request?

4. How do the people of Israel respond to God's deliverance?

5. Is Joash (Jehoash) of Israel a good king? Why or why not?

6. What prophecy does Elisha make to Joash of Israel on his deathbed?

7. What happens to the dead man who was cast into the grave of Elisha? What does this incident illustrate?

Lesson 157.
Amaziah vs. Jehoash: Israel defeats Judah
2 Chronicles 25

Note: *2 Chronicles parallels and includes 2 Kings 15, but also includes some additional information about Amaziah's reign.*

1. Is Amaziah a good king? Why or why not?

2. What doesn't he do that he should have done?

3. Does God approve of Amaziah's hiring of mercenary soldiers from Israel? Why not?

4. After the victory over the Edomites, what does Amaziah do that angers God?

5. Is Amaziah's challenge to Israel wise?

6. Who wins the battle between Israel and Judah? Why?

Lesson 158.
Azariah (Uzziah) & Jotham
2 Chronicles 26

1. Is Uzziah a good king? Why or why not?

2. What happens to Uzziah after he has become strong? What applications can we draw from this?

3. What happens to Uzziah when he goes into the temple to burn incense on the altar?

Lesson 159.
Jeroboam II, Zechariah, Shallum, Menahem, Pekahiah, Pekah, Hoshea.
2 Kings 14:23-29
2 Kings 15:8-31

Background: *In these few verses, we deal with the last seven kings of Israel. We will save a complete examination of the destruction of Israel under Hoshea for lesson 161. These seven kings cover a time span of only 60-65 years, with many of their reigns overlapping. Especially towards the end, it is apparent that, in Israel, moral anarchy has generated political instability as well.*

1. Is Jeroboam a good king? How does he become king? How long does he reign?

2. Is Zechariah a good king? How long does he reign?

3. Is Shallum a good king? How does he become king? How long does he reign?

4. Is Menahem a good king? How does he become king? How long does he reign?

5. Is Pekahiah a good king? How does he become king? How long does he reign?

6. Is Pekah a good king? How does he become king? How long does he reign?

7. How does Hoshea become king?
   More about Hoshea in lesson 161.

Background: *The prophet Jonah is mentioned in 2 Kings 14:25. The book of Jonah is one of the most intriguing of the prophetic books. Jonah lived during the reign of Jeroboam II and the book is about his reluctant mission to proclaim judgement, not to Israel, but to Ninevah. If you have time, this is the chronological place to read it.*

Hosea and **Amos**, prophets to Israel, are also dated during the reign of Jeroboam II. There are references to his kingship in both books - and none too flattering are the references!

*Of all the prophetic books, **Amos** is probably one of the most easily understood. Consider reading at least parts of it aloud to your children. It details the reasons why God HAS to judge Israel — and helps children to understand how wicked Israel has become.*

Lesson 160.
Jotham & Ahaz, Kings of Judah
2 Chronicles 27-28

Chapter 27

1. Is Jotham a good king? Does he follow in the footsteps of his father? Do the people follow his example?

2. Why does Jotham become mighty?

Chapter 28

3. Is Ahaz a good king? Why or why not?

4. What foreign gods does he worship?

5. How does he worship them? Has any other king of Judah done this?

6. What happens to Ahaz as a result of his wickedness?

7. What does the prophet Oded say to Israel as they bring in captives from Judah?

8. Who does Ahaz turn to for help when Edom attacks Judah?

9. Where is Ahaz buried?

10. Why isn't he buried with the other kings of Judah?

Background: *The prophet **Isaiah** proclaims God's judgement (and promises of restoration) to Judah. His message is similar to the one proclaimed in Israel by Joel, Hosea, and Amos. **Isaiah**'s message begins with a condemnation of the sins of Judah (and they are many). He prophesies concerning God's judgement, Judah's captivity and then ends with a vision of Judah's restoration. Much of what he has to say about a future deliverer for Judah concerned not just Judah's captivity, but man's captivity to sin. The deliverer would not just restore the political fortunes of Judah, but in God's own plan of salvation, he would be the Messiah, God's anointed one, to bring about the deliverance of all mankind.*

Lesson 161.
The Destruction of Israel by Assyria
2 Kings 17

1. Is Hoshea a good king? Why or why not?

2. What happens when Hoshea refuses to offer tribute to the king of Assyria?

3. Why is Israel defeated, taken captive, and dispersed by Assyria?

4. Has God warned Israel? How?

5. Has Judah kept God's commandments better than Israel?

6. Who does the king of Assyria bring to settle in Samaria?

7. What gods end up being served in the land given to the 10 Northern tribes?

Lesson 162.
Hezekiah Orders the Temple Cleansed
2 Chronicles 29

1. Is Hezekiah a good king? Why or why not?

2. What is the first recorded action by Hezekiah as king? Why is it significant that he does this first?

3. What does Hezekiah command the priests and Levites to do?

4. Why does Hezekiah want the temple to be cleaned?

5. What does Hezekiah do once the temple had been cleansed?

6. What songs does Hezekiah command to be sung?

   "Thus the service of the house of the LORD was established again."
   2 Chronicles 29:35

Lesson 163.
Hezekiah Celebrates Passover
2 Chronicles 30 - 31

Background: *Passover was supposed to be celebrated on the 14th day of the FIRST month, but Numbers 9:10-11 made provision for anyone who was unclean or on a distant journey on that day to celebrate Passover a month later on the 14th day of the SECOND month. This apparently is the tradition that Hezekiah and his princes appealed to since the priests and the temple had not been ready on the prescribed day.*

Chapter 30

1. Why is it significant that Hezekiah would culminate his reform and cleansing of the temple with a national celebration of Passover? What does Passover commemorate?

2. Why is it significant that Hezekiah would send his couriers to issue invitation to ALL of Israel (Dan to Beersheeba) rather than just Judah and Benjamin?

3. What is the reaction of the tribes of Israel to Hezekiah's invitation to come and celebrate the Passover at Jerusalem?

4. What do the crowds do in Jerusalem before the Passover celebration?

5. Many who were ritually unclean still partook of the Passover. How did Hezekiah react? What does he ask God to do?

   "So there was great joy in Jerusalem, because there was nothing like this in Jerusalem since the days of Solomon the son of David, king of Israel."
   2 Chronicles 30:26

Chapter 31

6. What do the people do after the Passover as they return home?

Background: *Verses 2-19 has to do with the reform and reestablishment of the offerings for the priests and the distribution of their portions. Pretty dry stuff, though an important part of Hezekiah's overall reforms.*

Verses 20-21 give a summary of Hezekiah's reforms of the temple and worship.

Lesson 164.
Hezekiah and the Siege of Jerusalem
2 Kings 18

We return now to Kings for an account of military events during Hezekiah's reign, after his reform of the temple.

1. Is Hezekiah a good king? Why or why not?

2. Shalmaneser, King of Assyria besieges Samaria — who wins?

3. Sennacherib, King of Assyria seizes the cities of Judah — what does Hezekiah do?

4. Rabshakeh comes to besiege Jerusalem — what does Hezekiah do?

5. What "deal" does Rebshakeh offer the people of Jerusalem? What does he repeatedly tell them NOT to do?

   "Has any one of the gods of the nations delivered his land from the hand of the king of Assyria?"

   2 Kings 18:33

6. How do you think God will respond to this challenge?

Lesson 165.
... the rest of story — Jerusalem Saved
2 Kings 19

1. What does King Hezekiah do when he heard Rebshakeh's taunt?

2. What message does the prophet Isaiah give to Hezekiah?

3. What happens to the Assyrian army?

4. What happens to Sennacherib, king of Assyria?

Lesson 166.
Hezekiah's Reprieve and Isaiah's Prophecy
2 Kings 20

1. Why does God add fifteen years to Hezekiah's life?

2. What sign does God provide to Hezekiah to confirm his extension of Hezekiah's life?

Background: *Assyria was the powerful state most feared at this time. Babylon was not yet a significant threat. Perhaps Hezekiah hoped for a favorable alliance. Perhaps he simply wanted to impress the Babylonians with his own wealth. In any event he showed them everything and Isaiah does not seem too pleased with the king's actions.*

3. What prophecy does Isaiah make to Hezekiah concerning everything he has shown the Babylonians?

Hezekiah's death and Manasseh's succession are going to reverse Judah's fortunes.

Lesson 167.
Manasseh and Amon, Wicked Kings
2 Chronicles 33
2 Kings 21

Background: *The story of Manasseh's change of heart after being taken captive by the Assyrians is found only in Chronicles. It is an important incident. On the other hand, the specific charge that Manasseh "shed very much innocent blood until he filled Jerusalem from one end to another" is found only in Kings. Both accounts are worth reading.*

1. Is Manasseh a good king? Why or why not?

2. What does he do that displeased God? How is he different from his father Hezekiah? *(You might want to reserve judgment until you read the entire account of his reign. He has a change of heart...)*

3. What does Manasseh do in the temple which his father had cleansed?

4. What judgement does God pronounce on Judah because of Manasseh?

5. What specific sin does God charge Manasseh with?

6. Who captures Manasseh? What do they do to him?

7. What did Manasseh do while a captive?

8. What does he do when he returns from captivity?
    After reading this passage, return to questions one and two.

9. Is Amon a good king? Why or why not?

10. What does he do? Is he like his father or different?

11. How does Amon die?

12. What do the people do to the servants who had killed Amon?

Background: *The prophet Nahum records his prophecy during the reign of Manasseh. His oracle is a denunciation of the Assyrians and their capital Ninevah. The LORD condemns the cruel practices of the Assyrians and announces that their capital city will be utterly destroyed. Just as Nahum had prophesied, Ninevah was destroyed by the combined armies of the Medes, Babylonians, and Scythians in 612 B.C.*

Lesson 168.
Josiah, Hilkiah, Repair the Temple
2 Chronicles 34

Background: *The account of Josiah in 2 Chronicles 34 is paralleled by the account in 2 Kings 22 with one exception. 2 Chronicles provides more detail about the beginning of his reforms as a young man.*

1. Is Josiah a good king? Why or why not?

2. What does he begin to do while still a youth?

3. What project does he tackle when he becomes eighteen?

4. What tribes does Josiah rule over as king of Judah?
    (or at least, which tribes contributed money towards rebuilding the temple?)

5. What is found during the rebuilding of the temple under Josiah and Hilkiah?

6. How does Josiah react to the reading of the law?

7. What does Josiah command Hilkiah to do?

8. What message does God deliver through Huldah the prophetess?

9. What does God promise he will do for Josiah concerning his judgement?

10. What covenant does Josiah make with God? Who does he include in the covenant?

11. What lessons can we draw from the life of Josiah? What applications can we make to our own lives?

Lesson 169.
Josiah Cleanses the Temple, Celebrates Passover
2 Kings 23

Background: *The account of Josiah's cleansing Israel of idolatry in 2 Kings 23 is paralleled somewhat in 2 Chronicles 35, but there the focus is more on the details of the celebration of the Passover. 2 Kings 23 provides more specific information on the idols and altars destroyed by Josiah, which is why we have preferred it as the account of the rest of his reign.*

1. What action does Josiah command after reading the book of the law?

2. Based on the list of places and gods which Josiah attacks, how widespread would you say the problem of idolatry is in Judah?

3. What is the significance of Josiah's destruction of the altar at Bethel which Jeroboam had made?

4. Why is the celebration of Passover by Josiah significant? (*cf. 2 Chronicles 35:16-19*)

5. How does Josiah die? *cf 2 Chronicles 35:20-27*

6. Who chants a lament for Josiah?

7. Is Jehoahaz a good king? Why or why not?

8. How long does he rule? What happens to him?

9. How does Jehoiakim become king?

10. Is Jehoiakim a good king? Why or why not?

11. Who really controls Judah?

Background: *The prophet **Jeremiah** receives his call during the reign of Josiah and continues his proclamations and prophecies until the eleventh year of Zedekiah, when the people of Jerusalem went into exile. **Jeremiah** was active during Josiah's reign and the revival associated with it and then again in the reigns of Jehoiakim and Zedekiah. His prophecies of God's coming judgement on Judah — her impending defeat and exile in Babylon — did not make him popular with the rulers of Judah. Chapter 35-39 especially contain some important historical narratives of events from the reigns of Jehoiakim and Zedekiah.*

Lesson 170.

Pharaoh & Nebuchadnezzar

2 Kings 24

1. Who places Jehoiakim on the throne?

2. Does Pharaoh Neco protect him when he rebels against Nebuchadnezzar?

3. Why, specifically, does God say that judgement is falling on Judah?

4. Is Jehoiachin a good king? Why or why not?

5. What happens when Jehoiachin goes out to meet Nebuchadnezzar?

6. How does Zedekiah become king?

7. Who really controls Judah?

Lesson 171.

Zedekiah rebels against Babylon

2 Kings 25

1. What happened when the king and the men of war attempt to flee Jerusalem?

2. What do the Babylonians do to Zedekiah?

3. What happens to the temple, the king's palace, and all the houses of Jerusalem?

4. When the people rebel against the Babylonian governor, Gedaliah, what happens?

5. Where do the rebels flee after killing Gedaliah?

6. What happens to King Jehoiachin?

Background: *The magnitude of the tragedy is hard to grasp. God's temple, and God's city were both destroyed with fire and his chosen people were led captive into exile. It is hard for us to imagine how devastating this must have been to those who sought to serve and follow God. Read **Psalm 137** for a glimpse of Judah's despair.*

Lesson 172.
Daniel in Captivity
Daniel 1

1. How does Daniel come to be in Babylon?

2. What are Daniel and the other youths commissioned to learn?

3. What part of Daniel's training does he object to?

4. What test does Daniel propose to evaluate his obedience to God?

5. How does God bless Daniel and his companions?

6. What position is given to Daniel and his companions?

This chapter gives a wonderful model for students to encourage them to apply themselves to their studies!

Lesson 173.
Daniel and Nebuchadnezzar's Dreams
Daniel 2

1. What does King Nebuchadnezzar want his wise men to do?

2. What is their reply to the king's request?

3. What is Daniel's reply to Arioch, the captain of the king's bodyguard?

4. Who does Daniel say can interpret the king's dream?

5. What is Nebuchadnezzar's response to Daniel's interpretation?

6. What position does Nebuchadnezzar give to Daniel?

7. What request does Daniel make of Nebuchadnezzar?

Background: *This begins a long tradition in Babylon of Jews serving in positions of authority and importance. From Daniel and his companions through Ezra, Esther and Mordecai, and Nehemiah.*

Lesson 174.
Daniel's Companions and the Fiery Furnace
Daniel 3

1. What does King Nebuchadnezzar command concerning the image of gold?

2. Why would this be a problem for the Jews in Babylon? Compare this with the practices of Israel and Judah which had brought about God's judgement!

3. What positions do Shadrach, Meshach, and Abednego hold in Babylon?

4. Do Shadrach, Mechach, and Abednego predict that God will save them from the furnace?

5. What happens to the men who threw Shadrach, Meshach, and Abednego into the furnace?

6. Who is with Shadrach, Meshach, and Abednego in the furnace?

7. What is King Nebuchadnezzar's response to Shadrach, Meshach, and Abednego's deliverance?

Background: *For a wonderful version of this story, see the World's Greatest Stories from the World's Greatest Book, Tape Number Three, by George Sarris. Mr. Sarris is a gifted actor and his retelling of the fiery furnace is exciting. Best of all, his script is nothing but the Bible text itself, word for word! (Available in both NIV and KJV.)*

Lesson 175.
Daniel and another Dream of the King
Daniel 4

This chapter is a very unusual part of the Bible. It was written by King Nebuchadnezzar himself!

1. Why does Nebuchadnezzar send for Daniel to interpret his dream?

2. What does the tree in Nebuchadnezzar's dream stand for?

3. What advice does Daniel give to Nebuchadnezzar in order that he might escape God's judgement?

4. What is King Nebuchadnezzar doing when God's judgement is executed?

5. What result does God's judgement have in King Nebuchadnezzar's life?

Lesson 176.
Belshazzar and the Handwriting on the Wall
Daniel 5

1. What kind of a party is King Belshazzar having?

2. Why does he have the gold and silver vessels from the temple brought to him?

3. Who reminds King Belshazzar about Daniel?

4. What does Daniel do with the gifts offered to him by King Belshazzar?

5. What is it about King Belshazzar that has displeased God?

6. What is God's judgement on King Belshazzar?

7. How does King Belshazzar react to Daniel's interpretation of the writing?

8. What happens to King Belshazzar?

Lesson 177.
Darius, Daniel, & the Lion's Den
Daniel 6

1. What position does Darius give to Daniel?

2. What do Daniel's rivals plot to do?

3. How does Daniel respond to Darius' decree?

4. How does Darius react to the news that Daniel has violated the decree? How does this compare to Nebuchadnezzar's reaction to Shadrach, Meshach, and Abednego's violation of his similar decree?

5. What does Darius say to Daniel as he is cast into the lion's den?

6. What did Darius do while Daniel was in the lion's den?

7. What happens to the men who have conspired and accused Daniel?

8. What does Darius decree?

Lesson 178.
Cyrus' Decree to Rebuild the Temple
Ezra 1, 2, 3

Background: *Given the fact of the service by Daniel and his companions to Nebuchadnezzar, Belshazzar, and Darius, it is not surprising to find their successor, King Cyrus should appeal to the LORD of heaven and announce that he had been appointed to rebuild the temple.*

Chapter 1

1. Who does Cyrus say has made him ruler over all the kingdoms of the earth?

2. What does Cyrus say God has appointed him to do?

3. Which tribes arise to return and give gifts for the building of the temple?

Chapter 2

4. How large is the assembly which set out to return to Jerusalem?

Chapter 3

5. What is the first thing done when the assembly returns to Jerusalem?

6. What are the two reactions among the assembly when the foundation of the temple is laid?

Lesson 179.
Opposition to rebuilding the temple
Ezra 4

1. What do the enemies of Judah and Benjamin ask to do?

2. How does Zerubbabel answer them?

3. What do the enemies of Judah and Benjamin do when their help is rejected?

4. What accusation do the enemies of Judah and Benjamin make about Jerusalem? In light of God's pronouncements and the history of Judah and Israel, why is this accusation ironic?

5. How does King Artaxerxes respond to the accusation?

Lesson 180.
Work on the Temple Resumed
Ezra 5 & 6

Chapter 5

1. Who resumes the work of rebuilding the temple?

2. What does the governor of the province do?

3. What defense do Zerubbabel, Jeshua, Haggai, and Zechariah make for rebuilding the temple?

Chapter 6

4. What does King Darius find when he searches the archives?

5. What instructions does Darius send to governor Tattenai?

6. Who does Darius say would pay for rebuilding the temple?

7. What is the first feast celebrated in the rebuilt temple after its dedication?

Background: *This is the period of the prophets Haggai and Zechariah (mentioned in the text). If you have time and interest, this is the appropriate place to read and study their message.*

Lesson 181.
Ahasuerus puts away his Queen
Esther 1

The book of Esther is one of our family's favorites. It is FULL of irony, suspense, humor, and danger. The good guys have to act with the greatest wisdom and shrewdness, and the bad guys are real bad guys who deserve to fall. And boy do we love to watch them get what's coming to them.

The feast of Purim is traditionally celebrated enthusiastically with costumes and parties, remembering the deliverance of God's people from certain annihilation. Esther celebrates the triumph of God's people over their enemies. Many Jewish families will also declare a "personal Purim" to celebrate times when they have seen God working His deliverance in their own lives. So Purim is a time when those of us who have been delivered from certain death by the Redeemer Jesus can celebrate and rejoice over our own salvation. We encourage you to research the customs surrounding the celebration of Purim and hold your own feast. And as you read the story to your children, have fun!

1. As the book of Esther opens, what is happening in Susa? Why? How is King Ahasuerus described? Would you expect him to be a modest, humble man? Why or why not?

Background: *Ahasuerus is also known in history by the name Xerxes. When you study the history of Ancient Greece, you will have opportunity to see another side of him as he is one of the Persian kings who attempts to conquer Greece. He appears in these other historical accounts as a fairly proud and foolish man. See if you think this assessment is consistent with the man you meet in the book of Esther.*

2. Why does King Ahasuerus send for Queen Vashti? Describe his condition when he calls for her. What exactly does Ahasuerus want Vashti to do?

Note: *Most commentators agree that Ahasuerus was asking Vashti to do more than say hello to all the nice people. It is generally understood that he was commanding Vashti to appear before the crowd (at the end of an evening of drinking) wearing her crown — and only her crown. Knowing this helps the children to understand that Vashti was not just being a difficult and cantankerous woman, and they tend to be as disgusted with the king as Vashti seems to have been.*

3. What was the King's initial reaction to Vashti's refusal to attend his banquet?

4. What do the King's advisors tell him he should do? Why? What is their motivation? What does the King do?

Maps: *Map # 15 in the **Student Bible Atlas** shows the extent of the Persian Empire.*

Lesson 182.
Esther and Mordecai please the King
Esther 2

1. Describe King Ahasuerus' attitude toward Vashti once his anger subsides? What applications might we draw from this about acting in the heat of anger?

2. How do the King's attendants attempt to resolve the problem? What do they suggest to the King?

3. To which tribe does Mordecai belong? How did they come to be in Susa?

4. What is his relationship to Esther? Why is he the one caring for Esther?

5. How would you describe Esther? What impression does she make on everyone who meets her? Why do you think this happens?

6. How do the eunuchs respond to Esther? What do they advise her? Does she listen? what does this show about her character?

7. What impression does Esther make on the king?

8. How does Mordecai show his loyalty to King Ahasuerus? What happens as a result of his actions? Is Mordecai rewarded here?

Lesson 183.
Mordecai angers Haman
Haman plots Revenge
Esther 3 & 4

1. Describe the relationship between Haman and Mordecai?

2. What does Haman resolve to do because of his rage at Mordecai?

3. What does Haman promise the King in return for the right to destroy a "certain people?"

4. What does Mordecai do when he learns of the decree which Haman has secured?

5. Why does Esther hesitate to approach the king about Haman's decree?

6. What rebuke does Mordecai make to Esther? Why does he say she has attained royalty? In what ways might we apply Mordecai's rebuke to our own lives?

7. What request does Esther make of Mordecai and all the Jews in Susa?

Lesson 184.

Esther appeals to the King
Esther 5

Background: *Don't overlook the drama in Esther waiting quietly and expectantly in her royal robes in the king's inner court. Since she has not been summoned, she does not know when Ahasuerus notices her whether he will hear her or sentence her to death.*

1. What is the first request Esther makes of King Ahasuerus when she is recognized?

2. What is the second request Esther makes of King Ahasuerus when he and Haman come to her banquet?

3. What is Haman's mood after the banquet with the king and queen? What is Haman's mood after he saw Mordecai?

4. What complaint does Haman make to his wife?

5. What solution does she propose?

Lesson 185.

The King Honors Mordecai Haman Outraged
Esther 6

Review the events of the previous chapter. Build the suspense. Above all, don't overlook the humor of the situation — Haman's self-absorbed ego, shattered as he discovers that the King wishes to honor his worst enemy, Mordecai. This chapter provides the perfect illustration of pride coming before a fall. Everyone loves watching Haman fall.

1. How does Mordecai's loyalty to the King come to the King's attention? How does the King respond?

2. Why does Haman come to see the king? Isn't it interesting that Mordecai's service to the King comes to the King's attention even as Haman comes to ask for Mordecai's life? Merely coincidence?

3. When the King says, "the man whom the king desires to honor..." who does Haman think the King is really talking about? How does his understanding of the words affect his answer?

4. Who does Haman have to honor? How do you think he feels about it?

5. What bit of helpful advice do Zeresh and the wise men have for Haman now?

You might consider acting this chapter out. Encourage the children to really imagine the emotions and responses portrayed in this chapter.

Lesson 186.
Haman's Plot Revealed, Haman Executed
Esther 7 & 8

This chapter is one of high drama and climactic revelation. Kids LOVE the sense of drama. Read this with suspense and drama.

Chapter 7

1. What does Esther ask for at the banquet she is giving for the king?
2. Who does she identify as "a foe and an enemy?"
3. What mistake does Haman make which increases the king's outrage?
4. Where is Haman executed? In what way is this especially fitting?

Chapter 8

5. How does Esther get the king to revoke the decrees?
6. What new decree did the king grant?

Background: *The holiday on which the Jews were given permission to destroy their enemies is celebrated and commemorated in the feast of Purim.*

Lesson 187.
The Jews Destroy their Enemies
Esther 9 & 10

1. What happens on the day that the Jews were supposed to have been destroyed?
2. What happens to Mordecai? How does his position change?
3. How many of their enemies do the Jews kill in Susa? in the provinces?
4. Do the Jews take any plunder from their enemies?
5. What does Mordecai command the Jews throughout the provinces of King Ahasuerus to do?
6. Why is Purim celebrated?
7. What position does Mordecai hold after these events?
8. What "personal Purims" might your family celebrate? Don't overlook the deliverance won for us by our Redeemer, Jesus.

Lesson 188.

Ezra appointed Governor by Artaxerxes

Ezra 7 & 8

Background: *Returning to the book of Ezra, we go one generation beyond Esther and Mordecai. King Ahasuerus (Xerxes) has been succeeded by his son, Artaxerxes. Ezra, a Levite, is commissioned by King Artaxerxes to return to Jerusalem.*

Chapter 7

1. How is Ezra described? What is his lineage? What is his education? What is his position with the king? Why?

2. What has Ezra set his heart on?

3. What authority does Artaxerxes give to Ezra?

Chapter 8

4. What does Ezra do at the river Ahava before leaving for Jerusalem?

Lesson 189.

The Problem of Foreign Wives

Ezra 9 & 10

Chapter 9

1. What problem does Ezra confront first in Jerusalem?

2. How does Ezra react to the news of mixed marriages?

3. What does Ezra acknowledge in his prayer to God concerning Judah's sin?

Chapter 10

4. How do the people react during Ezra's prayer?

5. What does Ezra say to the assembly of Judah and Benjamin?

6. What pledge do the people make to Ezra?

7. What steps do they take to demonstrate their repentance?

Lesson 190.
Nehemiah hears of Jerusalem's Distress
Nehemiah 1 & 2

Chapter 1

1. Where is Nehemiah?

2. What news does he hear of Jerusalem?

3. How does he react to the news?

4. What position does Nehemiah hold? What can you tell about his relationship to the king?

Chapter 2

5. What does Nehemiah do when the King asks him what his request is?

6. What request does he make? How does the King respond?

7. What does Nehemiah do first when he arrives at Jerusalem?

8. What was the reaction of Sanballat and Tobiah when Nehemiah began rebuilding the walls of Jerusalem?

You might find it helpful to list the actions of Nehemiah's opposition and Nehemiah's response to them. There is a progression and sequence here which has general application to all situations in which God's people face opposition.

The Jews Build
with one hand on their Weapons
Nehemiah 3 & 4

Chapter 3

Background: *Chapter three is a listing of all those involved in the rebuilding of the wall and the gates, with their names and the section of the wall they worked on. Think of it as an extended bronze plaque in a cathedral, memorializing those who gave gifts for its construction.*

Chapter 4

1. Who are the Samaritans and Sanballat? Who are Tobiah and the Ammonites? What is their lineage?

2. What do they say to those rebuilding Jerusalem?

3. How does Nehemiah respond?

4. What steps does Nehemiah take to prepare for an attack?

Lesson 192.

The Rich repent of
Oppressing the Poor
Nehemiah 5

1. What problem arises among the Jews?

2. What have the poor been doing in order to feed their families?

3. What steps does Nehemiah take to deal with the problem?

4. How do the people react to Nehemiah's decree?

5. What example does Nehemiah set as governor in his use of money?

Lesson 193.
Nehemiah Threatened, but the Wall is Completed
Nehemiah 6

1. What charge does Sanballat make about Nehemiah?

2. What advice does the "prophet" Shemaiah give to Nehemiah?

3. Why does Nehemiah not follow it?

4. What happened to Nehemiah's enemies when the wall was completed?

Lesson 194.
The Reading of the Law
Nehemiah 8

Background: *Yes, this is the same Ezra described in the book of Ezra - a Levite scribe and student of the law who returned from Babylon to Jerusalem.*

1. What books would have been included in the "book of the law of Moses?"

2. How do the people react to the reading of the law?

3. What do Nehemiah the governor, Ezra the priest and scribe, and the Levites do to console the people?

4. What festival does Israel celebrate after Ezra read the law?

Lesson 195.
Israel Repents
Nehemiah 9-10

Background: *We're closing in on the end of OT history. This chapter provides a convenient history of God's providential actions in caring for his chosen people.*

Chapter 9

1. What is the occasion of this assembly?

The rest of chapter 9 is the "Whereas" section to the oath in chapter 10:

WHEREAS the LORD God who chose Abram and brought him out from Ur...

WHEREAS Thou didst perform signs and wonders against Pharaoh...

WHEREAS Thou didst come down on Mount Sinai...

WHEREAS our fathers acted arrogantly...

WHEREAS they refused to listen...

WHEREAS they made for themselves a calf of molten metal...

WHEREAS Thou didst bring them into the land...

WHEREAS they became disobedient and rebelled...

Chapter 10

2. What do the people promise in their oath?

3. How do the things you've just read in these two chapters apply to your own life?

Chapters 11 and 12 are lists of those who settled in various cities of Israel.

Lesson 196.

Purifying Israel (again!)

Nehemiah 13

Background: *See Nehemiah 2:19 for an earlier reference to Tobiah the Ammonite and his attitude towards the rebuilding of Jerusalem. It was truly and doubly outrageous for the priest to have set aside a chamber for him inside the temple!*

1. What does Nehemiah do when he finds out what Eliashib the priest has done?

2. What does Nehemiah do when he discovers that the Levites have not been paid?

3. What does Nehemiah do when he discovers the Sabbath being profaned?

4. What does Nehemiah do when he discovers that some of the Jews had married women from Ashdod, Ammon, and Moab?

Afterward

It is appropriate that the Old Testament ends with an account of Nehemiah's struggle with Judah's disobedience. Only shortly before this we have seen the people of God weeping before the LORD, recognizing their own failings, grieving over their sins, and vowing to repent and return to faithfulness. Then Nehemiah returns from a visit to Babylon to discover that the same old sinful behaviors are thriving again in Judah. The people neglect the poor, the LORD, and His Sabbath. We see a man who has determined to live righteously crying out to God, asking Him to remember his faithfulness as he attempts to call an easily and enthusiastically distracted people back to righteousness.

I am reminded of Jesus as he weeps over the unbelief of Jerusalem (Luke 19:41). But mostly I am sobered by the shortness of memory. Just yesterday, it seems, and must have also seemed to Nehemiah, the people were reciting the history of God's love for and deliverance of Israel. They were also remembering the ways in which Israel failed, forgot and wandered away. And now so soon after seeing the Lord God bring them back to the land of their fathers, they are wandering away again.

How quickly they've forgotten!

I find myself wishing that I could leave it there, with those poor, sorry unredeemed sinners in the deep, dark past. But I know that the ability to forget what God has done is a human failing that we are all prone to. But it really isn't, "How easily they forgot." What we should say is, "How easily we forget..." "How easily I forget."

Reading the last chapter of the book of Nehemiah, I am reminded again of the importance of passing these things on to our children. Of making sure that the things God has done for us and in us are so much a part of who we are that our children do not have opportunity to forget.

Lesson 196.
Purifying Israel (again!)
Nehemiah 13
(continued)

Afterward

God said this about Abraham, "I know him, that he will command his children and his household after him, and they shall keep the way of the LORD, to do justice and judgement...(Genesis 18:19). In Deuteronomy 6, (the passage we've been known to call the homeschooling chapter) God makes it clear again, that he expects parents to pass these things on to their children, to keep the way of the Lord. But there is even more here:

5. Hear O Israel: the Lord our God is one Lord:

6. And thou shalt love the Lord thy God with all thine heart, and with all thy soul, and with all thy might.

7. And these words, which I command thee this day, shall be in thine heart:

8. And thou shalt teach them diligently unto thy children, and shalt talk of them when thou sittest in thine house, and when thou walkest by the way, and when thou liest down, and when thou risest up.

9. And thou shalt bind them for a sign upon thine hand, and they shall be as frontlets between thine eyes.

10. And thou shalt write them upon the posts of thy house, and on thy gates.

11. And it shall be, when the Lord thy God shall have brought thee into the land which he sware unto thy fathers, to Abraham, to Isaac, and to Jacob, to give thee great and goodly cities, which thou buildedst not,

12. And houses full of all good things, which thou filledst not, and wells digged, which thou diggedst not, vineyards and olive trees, which thou plantedst not; when thou shalt have eaten and be full;

13. Then beware lest thou forget the Lord, which brought thee forth out of the land of Egypt, for the house of bondage.

If we begin our application of this passage at verse 6, we will do well. We will surround our children with the Word of the Lord, and that will be good. But if we begin at verse 5, we will do much better. If our children can look at us and say, "My Mom and Dad loved the Lord our God with all their heart, and soul and strength," then the outward trappings of faith will have some meaning to them. If all our children can say is that we knew a lot about the Bible, we will not have fulfilled our responsibility to them. What we learn we can forget, those we love become a part of us.

It will be the same for our children. If they know a lot about the Bible, they can forget a lot about the Bible. But if we can help them begin with verse 5, and learn to love the Lord with all that they are, then their knowledge about him will bear the fruit of faithfulness. *It is our deepest desire for our children that our love for Jesus be "caught" by them. So that they, like, Nehemiah can stand when others are faithless.*

Postscript

We hope your study of the Old Testament and the history of Israel has been profitable. Because of the promises of scripture (and not the meager assistance of this guide) we're confident that the study of scripture is of great benefit to our children.

We hope also that over the course of this study, your children's appetites have been whetted for additional, continual study of God's word. We are unnecessarily intimidated and fearful about approaching God's word and reading it for our edification. Our fervent hope is that you and your children will realize that, while guides and commentaries may at times be helpful, you don't have to have ANYTHING in order to study scripture profitably. Are there times in which background information is useful? Of course. But the scriptures are generally straightforward and (surprise!) interesting, exciting, captivating.

Rob: I am very grateful to a long list of people for their assistance as I have worked on this guide. My thanks to Warren and Valerie Gardner who first challenged me and encouraged me to apply myself to the study of the Scriptures and to apply the Scriptures to my life. My thanks also to the members of the Davidson Christian Fellowship who encouraged me and urged me not to lose sight of the fact that the Scriptures and the Christian faith were imminently reasonable and worthy of trust. I also wish to thank Pete and Maria Sommer (and Eric and Debbie Hansen) and the Stanford graduate student small group which they led. In the midst of the cultural hurricane, they were a true safe haven to study and share together. I have similarly been challenged and encouraged by the publications from Precept Ministries in Chattanooga as they have worked to spread the news about inductive Bible study to the body of Christ.

Finally, a very special thanks to my wife Cyndy who is my very special Bible study partner. Much of this study grew out of times we have spent together studying the Scripture and teaching various Sunday school classes together. God knew what he was talking about when he observed that "it is not good for the man to be alone." Cyndy has been my best, most faithful critic and encourager. This study would be vastly inferior without her help.

I must also give a special word of thanks to our children who have been extremely patient with their distracted father over this summer. My apologies for the times I've growled rather than been understanding and my thanks for the days you have tiptoed past my door because "Dad's writing again!!!"

Cyndy: I owe more than I could ever tell to

— my parents, who communicated a love for the Word that drew me to it, and prepared the (only slightly stubborn) soil, I guess you could say.

— Pretty Aunt Kay, who taught me how to study the Word, brought me into the Kingdom and who, together with Ralph Norwood, trained my palate and gave me a lasting desire for strong meat.

— And of course Rob, (What do you say we sign up for another seventeen years...)

Cyndy and Rob: We both want to record a special thank you to the Greenleaf staff from the summer of 1994: Laurie, Trish, Larry, Joan, Melanie, Dee, Kelly, Rachel, and Dawn. Thanks for your patience with an absentee boss and for fielding all those phone calls asking, "Is the Old Testament Guide ready yet?"

And finally, our thanks to the homeschool community across all 50 states (and beyond!). This is not a book we would have written had it not been for repeated requests and encouragement from so many of you. Thank you for your patience and your votes of confidence.

This book is richer for the input of all these people, but as is always the case with projects, any faults and defects are not theirs, but ours.

Sources

We have relied on a number of sources over the course of writing this guide. Our mainstay has been my copy of the ***International Inductive Study Bible***. Its introductions, maps, and genealogical charts have been extremely helpful. I have also referred frequently to ***The Daily Bible***, the soft-cover edition of ***The Narrated Bible***, compiled by F. Lagard Smith. This remarkable Bible version (NIV) takes all the books of the Bible and rearranges them chronologically and divides them into 365 daily readings. Rob's copy of ***The New Bible Commentary: Revised*** published by Eerdmans and purchased through Inter-Varsity Press 21 years ago has gotten a great deal more dog-eared this year as has Cyndy's copy of ***The Matthew Henry Commentary***. Finally ***Chronological and Background Charts of the Old Testament*** by John H. Walton has been frequently consulted.

What do we believe?

Parents and teachers looking over this guide have a legitimate interest in the perspective of the authors, so here are our brief spiritual biographies:

Rob: I was baptized as an infant in the Episcopal church, confirmed at 12 in the Presbyterian Church, and then "went forward" and made a personal commitment to Jesus Christ as Lord and Savior at a lay renewal weekend at my Presbyterian church when I was 15. I was actively involved with Inter-Varsity Christian Fellowship at Davidson College and at Stanford University. Cyndy and I feel we have spent much of our married life together looking for a church home. We attended Menlo Park Presbyterian Church in California together (but also visited Ray Stedman's Peninsula Covenant Church). We attended Tabernacle Baptist Church in Norfolk, Virginia. While we lived in Oklahoma, we attended (and I was baptized at) Westport Mennonite Brethren Church in Collinsville. During our stay in Northern Virginia, we attended both Northern Virginia Mennonite Church and Truro Episcopal Church. From 1988 to 1997, I served as a deacon, elder, and adult Sunday School teacher at Grace Bible Church in Lebanon, Tennessee. We are currently attending Abundant Life Church in Mt.Juliet, Tennesee where I serve on the Board of Overseers. I have always been much more interested in the character of the local church and reasonably indifferent to denominational affiliations.

Cyndy: I became a Christian at the very end of my senior year in high school as I attended a Bible study led by Kay Arthur. Kay taught me how to study the Bible, and the more I studied the more I became aware of my need and desire to truly know that I knew the Lord Jesus. How grateful I am to both Kay for being my first teacher, and to Ralph Norwood, my first pastor — their commitment to teaching the Word sparked the desire to "go deeper."

I was involved in Inter-Varsity Christian Fellowship — at Queens College in Charlotte, N.C. (and though I swore I'd never marry a "Davidson boy," here I am.) and at the University of Virginia. While, like Rob, I am most interested in the witness of an individual church body, it was in Charlottesville that I first discovered a "theological home," among Mennonite believers there. Over the past ten years I've worked primarily with the junior high aged young people, in church-based programs and leading a weekly teen Bible study in our home.

We both affirm the historic creeds of the church in their entirety and think their summary of a saving faith hard to improve on. We also believe the Scriptures to be the inspired, infallible, authoritative word of God but we are cautiously aware that faith in the Scriptures is not what saves, rather it is faith in the Lord Jesus Christ. We are thoroughly convinced that if one will faithfully follow the lordship of Christ, He will lead us into truth concerning his Word.

"All scripture is inspired by God and profitable for teaching, for reproof, for correction, for training in righteousness; that the man of God may be adequate, equipped for every good work."

2 Timothy 3:16-17

"And these words which I am commanding you today, shall be on your heart; and you shall teach them diligently to your sons and shall talk of them when you sit in your house and when you walk by the way and when you lie down and when you rise up."

Deuteronomy 6:6-7

A Few Words About Greenleaf Press

Greenleaf Press was founded by Rob & Cyndy Shearer in 1989. It was born of their frustration in searching for a history program for their children that was at the same time challenging, interesting, and historically accurate. What they were looking for was a curriculum that would begin at the beginning and present history in a logical, readable, chronological way. None of the available, in-print programs satisfied them. They discovered that the best history books for children they could find were, sadly, out of print. The best of the out-of-print classics were really terrific. They told interesting stories about real people. And the Shearer's discovered that their children loved history when it was presented in the form of an interesting story about a real person.

And so, they founded Greenleaf Press — to bring back to life some of the wonderful biographies which had been used to teach history so successfully in the past. The reprinting of Famous Men of Greece and Famous Men of Rome were Greenleaf's first publications. Those two books have now been joined by the reprint of Famous Men of the Middle Ages, Famous Men of the Renaissance and Reformation (written by Rob Shearer), The Greenleaf Guide to Old Testament History (written by Rob and Cyndy Shearer), and The Greenleaf Guide to Ancient Egypt (written by Cyndy Shearer).

Shortly after reprinting Famous Men of Rome, faced with questions from many people who liked the *Famous Men* books, but wanted help in HOW to use them, they decided to publish Study Guides showing how to integrate biographies, activities, and reference material. There are *Greenleaf Guides* available for Rome, Greece, and the Middle Ages, all written by Rob & Cyndy Shearer.

From that day to this, Greenleaf Press has remained committed to "twaddle-free", living books. We believe that history is both important and exciting and that our kids can share that excitement. We believe that if our children are to understand the roots of our modern-day, mixed-up world, they must study history. We're also thoroughly convinced that studying history with our children provides us with a wonderful opportunity to reflect with them on moral choices and Godly character.

Teaching History with Greenleaf Press Curriculum

Seven Year Plan
Year 1 — Old Testament (Historical Books: Genesis – Kings)
Year 2 — Egypt (& Old Testament Review)
Year 3 — Greece and Rome
Year 4 — The Middle Ages and The Renaissance
Year 5 — The Reformation and The Seventeenth Century (to 1715)
Year 6 — 1715 to 1850
Year 7 — 1850 to The Present

Six Year Plan
Year 1 — Old Testament and Egypt
Year 2 — Greece and Rome
Year 3 — The Middle Ages and The Renaissance
Year 4 — The Reformation to 1715
Year 5 — 1715 to 1850
Year 6 — 1850 to The Present

Five Year Plan
Year 1 — Old Testament, Egypt, Greece & Rome
Year 2 — The Middle Ages and The Renaissance
Year 3 — The Reformation and The Seventeenth Century (to 1715)
Year 4 — 1715 to 1850
Year 5 — 1850 to The Present

Four Year Plan
Year 1 — Old Testament, Egypt, Greece & Rome
Year 2 — The Middle Ages, The Renaissance, and The Reformation
Year 3 — 1600 to 1850
Year 4 — 1850 to The Present

Internet: www.greenleafpress.com
3761 Highway 109 N., Unit D
Lebanon, TN 37087
615-449-1617

greenleaf
P·R·E·S·S

Teaching History with Living Books
An overview of
GREENLEAF PRESS
Study Guides and History Packages

The Greenleaf Guide to Old Testament History

We are strongly persuaded that the history of Israel ought to be the first history studied by every child. This Guide outlines a daily reading program that works through all of the historical books of the Old Testament. The focus is on history — not theology. What is remarkable is that the historical books of the Bible always focus on a central character. The pattern of history in the Old Testament is built around a series of biographies and character studies. The Old Testament really could be subtitled "Famous Men of Israel." Thus, the Study Guide discussion questions focus on "What actions of this person are worthy of imitation?" "What actions should we avoid?" "What is God's judgment on this life?"

The 196 readings are intended to be used, one each day throughout the school year. Yes, we know that's a few more readings than most people have school days. Be creative. You could do more than one reading on some days, or you could continue the study into the summer or the next school year. The readings are designed to give the student (and parent/teacher) an overview of the history of Israel and an introduction to the key figures whose lives God uses to teach us about Himself and His character. These stories are intended for children in the elementary grades, and should be accessible, even to children in kindergarten or first grade (though they make a rich study for older children, even teens and adults)! If this seems surprising, the reader is reminded that God's plan for families is for fathers to teach these stories to their children. When God decrees in Deuteronomy 6:6-7 that "you shall teach them diligently to your sons and shall talk of them when you sit in your house and when you walk by the way and when you lie down and when you rise up," He is not referring to math facts and grammar rules. God's textbook for children are the stories from the Old Testament. He is specifically referring to the story of the Exodus from Egypt, but by implication He means the entire Old Testament. The Old Testament is God's textbook for children. This is the only textbook, quite probably, Jesus used during his education in the house of his parents. *Duration: One full academic year*

The Greenleaf Guide to Ancient Egypt

Ever wonder how Biblical history and Ancient Egypt fit together? Why was God so angry with Pharaoh anyway? This makes a perfect second history unit for students. Or, as an alternative, you could pause in your study of Old Testament history and study Egypt after you have finished the story of Joseph at the end of the book of Genesis. This unit has ten lessons, including one devoted to the rediscovery of Egypt and the development of the science of archaeology in the 19th century. There is also a lesson on the Exodus in the context of Egyptian culture. The main text for the study is the Landmark book, The Pharaohs of Ancient Egypt, which includes biographies of the following Pharaohs:

Cheops (builder of the Great Pyramid)
Hatshepsut (His Majesty, Herself!)
Thutmose III (the Napoleon of the
 Ancient World)

Aknaton (the monotheistic Pharaoh)
Tutankamon (the boy-Pharaoh)
Rameses II (Smiter of the Asiatics)
Duration: approximately 15 weeks

Famous Men of Greece

If you were to have asked a citizen of ancient Greece to tell you something about the history of his nation, he would have wanted to begin at what he would have considered to be the beginning. He would have begun by telling you about his gods and the myths and legends told about them. Even though the events described in the myths did not actually happen in the way the story says, the Greek myths will tell you much about what was important to the people who told them.

Greek culture forms the backdrop to all the events of the New Testament. Paul was educated not just in the teachings of the Rabbis, but also in the writings of the Greeks. He was able to quote from literature in his speech to the men of Athens. Many of the details in his letters become richer and more significant when understood in the context of Greek culture.

Famous Men of Greece covers the following chapters:

Introduction: the Gods of Greece
Deucalion and the Flood
Cadmus and the Dragon's Teeth
Perseus
Hercules and His Labors
Jason and the Golden Fleece
Theseus
Agamemnon, King of Men
Achilles, Bravest of Greeks
The Adventures of Odysseus

Lycurgus
Draco and Solon
Pisistratus the Tyrant
Miltiades the Hero of Marathon
Leonidas at Thermopylae
Themistocles
Aristides the Just
Cimon
Pericles
Alcibiades
Lysander

Socrates
Xenophon
Epaminondas and Pelopidas
Philip of Macedonia
Alexander the Great
Demosthenes
Aristotle, Zeno, Diogenes, Apelles
Ptolemy
Pyrrhus
Cleomenes III
Duration: approximately 15 weeks

Famous Men of Rome

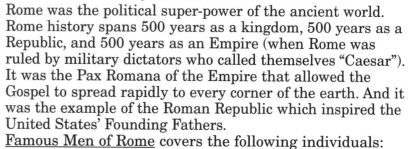

Rome was the political super-power of the ancient world. Rome history spans 500 years as a kingdom, 500 years as a Republic, and 500 years as an Empire (when Rome was ruled by military dictators who called themselves "Caesar"). It was the Pax Romana of the Empire that allowed the Gospel to spread rapidly to every corner of the earth. And it was the example of the Roman Republic which inspired the United States' Founding Fathers.

Famous Men of Rome covers the following individuals:

Romulus
Numa Pompilius
The Horatii and the Curiatii
The Tarquins
Junius Brutus
Horatius
Mucius the Left-Handed
Coriolanus
The Fabii
Cincinnatus
Camillus
Manlius

Manlius Torquatus
Appius Claudius Caecus
Regulus
Scipio Africanus
Cato the Censor
The Gracchi
Marius
Sulla
Pompey the Great
Julius Caesar
Cicero
Augustus

Nero
Titus
Trajan
Marcus Aurelius
Diocletian
Constantine the Great
End of the Western Empire

Duration: approximately 15 weeks

Famous Men of the Middle Ages

We come to a time when the power of Rome was broken and tribes of barbarians who lived north of the Danube and the Rhine took possession of the lands that had been part of the Roman Empire. These tribes were the Goths, Vandals, Huns, Franks and Anglo-Saxons. From the mixture of Roman provinces, Germanic tribes, and Christian bishops came the time known as The Middle Ages and the founding of the European nation-states.

Famous Men of the Middle Ages covers the following individuals:

The Gods of the Teutons
The Niebelungs
Alaric the Visigoth
Attila the Hun
Genseric the Vandal
Theodoric the Ostrogoth
Clovis
Justinian the Great
Two Monks: Benedict and Gregory
Mohammed
Charles Martel
Charlemagne
Harun-al-Rashid
Egbert the Saxon

Rollo the Viking
Alfred the Great
Henry the Fowler
Canute the Great
El Cid
Edward the Confessor
William the Conqueror
Gregory VII & Henry IV
Peter the Hermit
Frederick Barbarossa
Henry the Second and His Sons
Louis the Ninth
St. Francis and St. Dominic
Robert Bruce

Marco Polo
Edward the Black Prince
William Tell
Arnold Von Winkelried
Tamerlane
Henry V
Joan of Arc
Gutenberg
Warwick the Kingmaker

Duration: approximately 15 weeks (though many families supplement this study with literature readings and extend it to a full year).

Famous Men of the Renaissance and Reformation

The Middle Ages were not the "Dark Ages." Yet there had been substantial changes in Europe from 500 to 1300 AD. Rome and her Empire fell. The Germanic tribes moved into the old Roman provinces and established feudal kingdoms. Many of the Roman cities declined in population or were abandoned. Gradually, much of the literature and learning of the classical world was lost and forgotten. Around 1300, in the towns of northern Italy especially, a group of men began to devote themselves to the recovery and revival of the classical world.

As the men of the Renaissance completed their work of recovery, another group of men arose, devoted to reform of the abuses within the church and relying upon the texts and tools of scholarship developed by the Renaissance humanists. The Protestant Reformation marks the beginning of "modern" European history. During that time we see men and women of remarkable courage and ability devoted to restoring the church to Biblical patterns. There are triumphs and virtues to be imitated, and tragedies and vices to be avoided.

Famous Men of the Renaissance and Reformation covers the following individuals:

Renaissance
Petrarch
Giotto
Filippo Brunelleschi and Donatello
Lorenzo Valla
Cosimo D' Medici
Lorenzo D' Medici
Girolamo Savonarola
Sandro Botticelli
Leonardo Da Vinci
Cesare Borgia

Niccolo Machiavelli
Leo X (Giovanni De Medici)
Albrecht Durer
Michelangelo Buonarroti
Erasmus
Reformation
John Wyclif
Jan Hus
Martin Luther
Charles V
Ulrich Zwingli
Thomas Muntzer

Conrad Grebel & Michael Sattler
Melchior Hoffman, Jan Matthys & Menno Simons
Henry VIII
Thomas More
William Tyndale
Thomas Cromwell & Thomas Cranmer
John Calvin
John Knox

Duration: Approximately 15 weeks.

Graphical Timeline of Ancient History

by Robert G. Shearer
© 1996 Greenleaf Press

Key Dates

Israel

c.1900 B.C. –	Joseph sold into slavery
c.1445 B.C. –	The Exodus
c.1000 B.C. –	Death of Saul, David becomes King
605-1344 B.C. –	The Exile

Egypt

2500 B.C. –	Khufu (Cheops) The Great Pyramid
1505-1484 B.C. –	Queen Hatshepsut
1361-1344 B.C. –	Amenhotep IV also known as Akhenaton
51-31 B.C. –	Cleopatra

Greece

c.1200 B.C. –	Siege of Troy
478-404 B.C. –	Civil War between Athens & Sparta
356-323 B.C. –	Alexander

Rome

753 B.C. –	Founding of Rome
509 B.C. –	Founding of the Roman Republic
100-44 B.C. –	Julius Caesar
312-327 A.D. –	Constantine
410 A.D. –	Sack of Rome by the Visigoths
476 A.D. –	Death of the last Roman Emperor

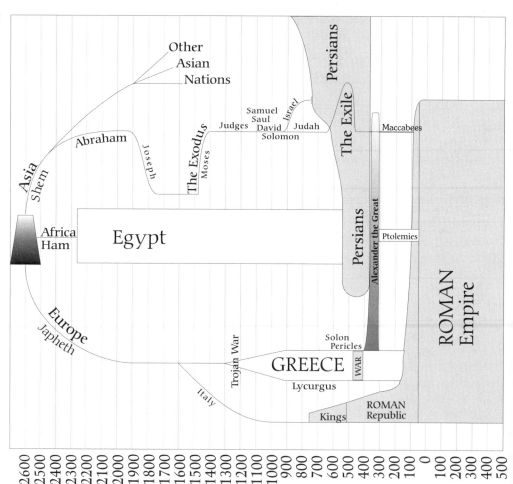

Graphical Timeline of Medieval History

Key Dates

England:

c.400 –	Romans withdraw
793 –	Sack of Lindisfarne by Vikings
871-899 –	Alfred the Great
1066 –	Norman Conquest
1339-1453 –	Hundred Years War
1455-1485 –	War of the Roses

France:

482-511 –	Clovis
714-41 –	Charles Martel
768-814 –	Charlemagne
1180-1223 –	Philip II Augustus
1412-1431 –	Joan of Arc

Germany:

936-937 –	Otto I, the Great
1152-90 –	Frederick I Barbarossa
1210-50 –	Frederick II, Stupor Mundi
1493-1519 –	Maximilian
1516-1556 –	Charles V

Italy:

440-461 –	Pope Leo I
480-543 –	St. Benedict
590-640 –	Pope Gregory
1073-85 –	Pope Gregory
1200-1240 –	St. Francis
1309-1378 –	Babylonian Captivity (of the Papacy)
1378-1417 –	The Great Schism
1096 –	1st Crusade
1147 –	2nd Crusade
1189 –	3rd Crusade